BETRAYAL TRAUMA

Karen Kellock Ph.D.

Manual for Superior Men

This is a complete theory based on Einstein physics, Political Psychology, Systems Theory and Archetypal Psychiatry.

FORMULA

All success attraction
All disease obstruction
All recovery elimination

You must fast on all three

OBSTRUCTIONS:

People
Habit
Food

BETRAYAL TRAUMA

If you've been in just one sick relationship it acts as a relational template.   The clown doesn't deserve a conversation but here you're kneeling before him, even begging him.   Without knowledge a black sheep begins a roller coaster of targetings and life changes suddenly. It's not that she's a narc-magnet but a loss of queen status creates toleration for maggots.

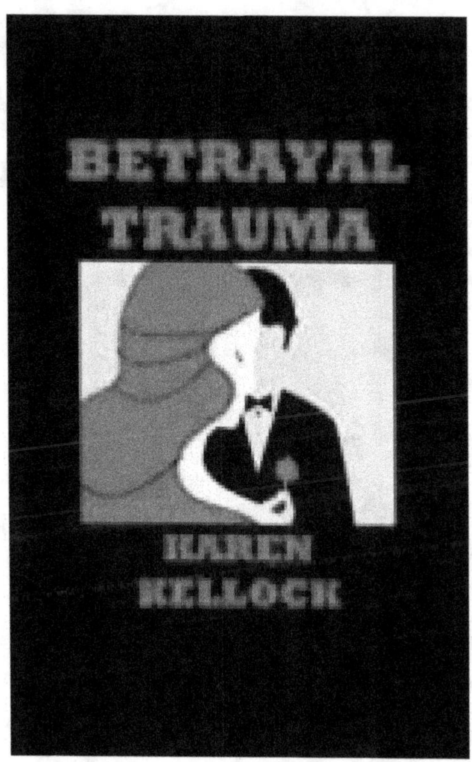

BETRAYAL TRAUMA

BETRAYAL TRAUMA

DON'T ENTERTAIN CREEPS IN YOUR HOUSE
WOMEN FERTILIZE MALE DISRESPECT
WOMEN FERTILIZE MISOGONY
HONOR MEN WHO HONOR YOU
MORE ABOUT CREEPING MEN
SILLY WOMEN GIVE IN
CLOWNS LEAVE WOUNDS
CHASTITY BRINGS DISCERNMENT
SEEK MEN WHO RESPECT VALUE
NARCISSISTS AND DISREGULATION
LONGTERM CONSEQUENCES OF BEING HATED
HE'S JUST A DIRTY OLD MAN
EXPERIENCE MAKES YOU RELATABLE
TRAUMA BONDING WITH NARCISSISTS
SHAMING INTO A YES PERSON
APPROVAL OF AN INFERIOR CIRCLE
TO WIN THE RACE, SEPARATE
THE BEST CHOOSES THE WORST
DEMONIC ENERGY IGNORED
LOST CONNECTION TO THE SELF
FALSE FEMALE FRIENDS
DISTANCE, BOUNDARIES, CONVERSATION
FRIEND OR CLIENT?
BECOME EMOTIONALLY IMPERVIOUS
TRAPPED AND GOING NOWHERE
LOVE STARVED WOMEN FALL IN
LOVE BOMBING TO BRING A FALL
GOD RESCUES US FROM TOXICITY
EMOTIONAL UNAVAILABILITY

BETRAYAL TRAUMA

BLINDED BY SEX AND ROMANCE
NO CONNECTEDNESS
SHALLOW CONVERSATION
TO WALK OUT FIRST WAKE UP
HEART GOTTA BREAK TO HEAL
INSANE LOVE IS TRAUMA BOND
DYSFUNCTIONAL FAMILIARITY
REPENTANCE = BACK TO GOD'S GRACE
MOVE AWAY FROM SOUL TIES
FEED SOUL WITH GOD'S WORD
THOUGHTS OF THE DAY
RELATIONSHIP DESTRUCTION
TOXIC LEGACIES
CODEPENDENCY
BETRAYAL TRAUMA
LIGHT'S OUT, TERROR IN THE GUT
FLYING MONKEYS
FEELING OF ZERO LOYALTY
GET INTO YOUR OWN THING
PEOPLE-WORSHIP
WIVES OF PORN ADDICTS BECOME SUICIDAL
DARK NIGHT OF THE SOUL (I KNOW IT WELL)
BETRAYAL TRAUMA SURVIVORS
PORN IS CHEATING
AFTER BETRAYAL TRAUMA
MESSY DISORDERLY HOMES
BT: AN ONSLAUGHT OF BIOCHEMISTRY
NOTHING IS SACRED TO THEM
WAITING FOR THE NEXT SHOE TO DROP
A SINGLE LIE DISCOVERY LEADS TO MYSTERY

BETRAYAL TRAUMA

REJECT THOSE WHO MINIMIZE PORN
NEED SAFETY TO BUILD INTIMACY
MORE ON NARCISSISTS
THEY CAN'T HIDE WHO THEY ARE
CRUELIANS
SINS ARE MAL-ADAPTIVE COPING DEVICES
PERVERSE TRIANGLES/SECRET ALLIANCES
THE BLIND INSIST THEY CAN SEE
TAKE CONTROL: DELETE FOOLS/CHOOSE FOLKS
LIVING WITH A RATTLESNAKE
DETACH FROM THE OUTER
DARE TO DISAPPOINT DEMANDERS
CREEPY CRUELIANS ONLY BRING YOU DOWN
THEY ARE EITHER "IN" OR "OUT"
DETACH THROUGH A SECRET WORLD
THE DEVIL'S CROWD IS POLITICALLY CORRECT
ENDING WITH NO FRIENDS IS BEST
BAD FAITH IN USELESS PEOPLE
HOME CENTER SOLUTION: SOLITUDE
YOUR ESSENCE IS YOUR PRIVATE CASTLE
GROUPS MAD AT ME: LOYALTY OR AUTONOMY?
PUTTING FAITH WHERE IT BELONGS
CRUELIANS LOVE PUTTING YOU IN FEAR
HARD-HEARTED ARE MISERABLE/CRUEL ARE LOST
CAREFUL OF EVIL HELPERS
STRIFE IS A KILLER
SPIN DOCTORS AND PLASTIC SURGEONS
NOT MULTICULTURAL, ONE BIG BROWN BLOB
SUPERIOR PAST TIMES
YOU'LL MOVE RIGHT ON
HIX POLITIX: BLAME IT ALL ON US
THUGS BRINGING US TO CRISIS

BETRAYAL NOTES

You should avoid any group that disrespect you even if some of the members are fine.

He doesn't know what you're talking about nor does he care. He's a narcissist but nothing rare.

They need you like water in a dry land for there's a mental DROUGHT the bible has said.

There's worlds inside waiting to be discovered but people try to divert you to the social order.

If they haven't invited you back it's a sign of the times sadly for they hate all truth and novelty.

Stop complaining about your problems. Most don't care and the rest are glad you got em.

EMOTIVISM

Emotivism: political views not driven by facts but internal emotions and they STAY like that.

Any inner contradiction seeks resolution and that is the function of the theoretician.

Jesus Christ saved me from everything that coulda happened so He can save this nation.

Emotivism allows one to attribute malicious intent to the opposition, a fact-ignoring reason.

They see you as evil cuz you think that way. Malicious intent: ignore all she has to say.

Emotivism: the only reason we disagree is because I'm a good and you're a bad person.

BETRAYAL NOTES

Understand the whole social generation: they don't come unless they bring their friends.

Emotivism: I love these people and you should too and you're just plain evil if you refuse to.

RULED BY EVIL CHILDREN

We're increasingly ruled by evil children who see "NO" as abuse and respond with VIOLENCE.

Communism: No one stands out and they hate anyone who does--that's the evil human condition.

Any novelty or counter-narrative is also seen as evil and thus a roadblock to creativity too.

Cancel culture is the antithesis of democracy: another contradiction of the left see.

He doesn't care what you have to say and never will, he's one of those narcissists/no thrill.

They beat me up cuz I was too smart for them: in comparison a direct contradiction.

Everyone across the world is craving normalcy and no one's providing it save Trump see.

NOTES ON BODY SENSITIVITY

Life is a pie so you decide: purify the diet or be wiped out by total load and sensitive to all of it.

Purify the diet or be sickened by cat dander. It's a budget so you decide cat lover.

Had an urge for shrimp, delicious. Then all night the pet dander made me sickened.

They urged me to eat beef and I did. Eyebags the next morning and total load way up: failed.

BETRAYAL NOTES

Eye bags indicate kidney dysfunction. Who needs this, all for you to lose weight I reckon'?

When reacting to chemicals you need a doctor who gets you on the treadmills: you go under.

A treadmill of tests, pills and feeling sick or taking hold of your life and investigating the prix?

Hard to trust professional men whether your doctor or estate lawyer. Take control or go under.

They charge you what they've found you have. Hide it or be gouged until you're dead.

The med profession never pins it on chemicals, it's always something wrong with you rascal.

They never pin it on chemicals but want you on theirs: a buncha face-bloaters and no-nos.

You're sick from chemicals. Doctor puts you on more. You don't recognize yourself anymore.

BETRAYAL TRAUMA

THE WORLD DEGRADES SELF-WORTH

To fight against a world's undertow you must apply deep thought to your worth and keep it there.

They hear gossip, believe it and tuck it away. Thus we go to God for our self-esteem boost ok?

I have to find the good in me because the world is conditioned to ignore the positives see.

You lose 100 lbs. and world says "you have loose skin". Ignore positives, put you down again.

They ignore positives then inflate negatives and we're trained to do the same: what a predicament.

I am fearfully and wonderfully made and that my soul knows well. Shut out world/get tough shell.

You've never been into you. Make a list of your greatest qualities and then the world's reaction too.

RELOCATE TO ESCAPE

Just relocate, put a fence up and you're free. Stuck in a past matrix they're still coming around see.

I wanted solitude in nature. The only way was to take what's there--by a tiny cabin I was honored.

It's easy to slide back so train yourself to think deeply about your worth: a stand alone original sir.

Make a list of your attributes to remind yourself cuz if you don't they'll pull you down no doubt.

BETRAYAL TRAUMA

You have to know your own worth, not allow the world to say you're a grasshopper or worse.

As he says in his heart so is he: your life materializes around that very template of YOU see.

DAILY DECLARE WORTH FIRST

You must daily declare this view of self so you're ready when the world comes in with insults.

What are you thinking about yourself and what are you saying to yourself: is it heavenly or to hell?

Allow NO bootie calls with your ex. Of all the crap going on these days this is the worst that it gets.

You should be constantly talking self up since the world is emptying your self-esteem nonstop.

One word and they empty out all of your confidence: Evil hearts in a generation of snakes.

I am valuable, I am irreplaceable. With these in your heart it then materializes and is irrevocable.

Daily declarations put you on stage to do what you were born to, not slip back into fear/feeling blue.

Run around trying to find one who will say you're fine when you shoulda said that early to thine.

VISION BRINGS RESTRAINT

Your vision of self's mission keeps you constrained but without a vision we are all over the place.

Define your vision as an individual and then you will see who fits and who doesn't that you know.

BETRAYAL TRAUMA

Without a constraining vision they connect to whatever is close to provide self-esteem to the low.

Without a constraining vision we never locate our sense of purpose and then nuts hang around us.

What's ahead is more important than behind. Focus on future and the past gets small/no big thing.

SELF-LOVE DEMANDS VISION

Self-love demands you define an individual vision or you're a rudderless ship hit from all directions.

It builds self-esteem when you know where you're going, taking power from others you're seeking.

When you know where you're going you know when someone's stopping you: this is valuable too.

Now you can transcend the moment, moving into your destiny and never anchored by your history.

Determine the requirements for a person to participate in your life. No more letting in smut/strife.

Now you're tough: No more letting people invade your house or allowing em in to use your stuff.

CONSTRAIN: DON'T LET EM IN

Don't let anyone in. If they can't meet standards they don't get in: your sanctuary isn't a trash bin.

They'd knock on the door and I'd let em in outa fear they'd call me unloving, inhospitable, a hater.

How I hated my unwanted guests and the interruption from what I do best yet I endured the pests.

BETRAYAL TRAUMA

Nothing shows disgustingly low self-worth as much as you allowing unvetted invaders on your turf.

That's YOUR space and you are highly affected by people good or bad ok? Tell them to go away.

Define your vision as an individual, not including anyone else. Now find the one and see if he fits.

RUBIES AND THE VIRTUOUS WOMAN

A virtuous woman: her price is far beyond rubies. Determine the requirements and be choosy.

You determine requirements for a man's access to your house, life and body or there's hell to pay.

He doesn't get to come in and out and bring all his friends and act like it's his, no way man.

You determine he must recognize a star, be a husband, ask to marry you and take you to the altar.

No warm up dinners in a row then it's all bootie calls. Come on, get some class/demand it from all.

First I was in the crazy cities for decades then to the desert wilderness but spoilers still came ok.

When A.A. seems like a liberal social club you've had it bud especially if a healing conservative.

You gotta keep telling yourself you're good/kind or the undertow drags you down, losing your mind.

They project their crap on you because the dumbed can't see above it. It is best to avoid it.

If he dithers/does not want to marry, move on. Life is tough and you need someone to count on.

BETRAYAL TRAUMA

SETTLING/THRILLED WITH NOTHING

You've allowed the guy with aluminum foil around his head to run in or out of your life instead.

They gotta be respectful, they gotta be loyal. Once you see they're not they're outa here girl.

Self-love weeds losers out by determining requirements. Are you unequally yoked? You decide that.

You weed em out before even being considered. You gotta be like this/stop being so desperate.

Self-love is achieved thru intentional solitude. I call this my office hours where no one intrudes.

You train yourself to love you. Learning to love yourself comes from putting self first--in solitude.

Be still and know that I am God. Then learn to be happy with me/myself and I despite flaws.

Soon you evolve into an individual who is independent. This is your highest destiny so enjoy it.

Put these things together and love the unique person in the mirror for on earth there is no other.

Stop looking for outer confirmers to do what you're capable of doing for yourself: that's superior.

SILLY WOMEN

They creep into houses leading captive silly women laden with sins/led away by diverse lusts.

Abuse leaves a woman broken for a season, a silly woman is a recurring volunteer for abusin'.

BETRAYAL TRAUMA

She moves from victim to seer [self-awareness/no repeat] but a silly woman is a serial volunteer.

She moves from being broken from abuse, to outright silliness by who she lets in her house too.

SILLY UNTIL HER FIFTIES

Abused in her 20s she's fifty and a silly lady, dealing with the same stuff from the seventies.

She reads one book after another but remains silly. She's just silly when it comes to men see.

Silly defined: having or showing a lack of common sense or judgement. To be absurd, weak, foolish.

To be silly means to be ridiculous/irrational. What does the bible say about Silly Woman Syndrome?

Silly women ever learning things they never apply—they're destroyed for lack of knowledge, aye.

Mostly she lacks knowledge because she rejected it. The queen of the footnotes never applies it.

Women: hundreds of books and teaching videos yet still they remain unactualized as individuals.

BREAKDOWNS OVER LITTLE MEN

So she's having a nervous breakdown over a little man who cheats constantly: she's just silly.

The number one silly position any woman can take: She's gonna make that man love her ok.

To feel you can spend enough money on people to make them loyal. This is not queenlike or royal.

BETRAYAL TRAUMA

The silly women actually think if they're good enough at sex they can force love even from an ex.

Many women pray for his love. God doesn't force us to love him let alone warming up some man.

LIFE IS A LADDER: UPHILL NOW

Life is a ladder so we're going all uphill now. We're not going back down to acting so unlike God.

A person not equally yoked or on the same frequency does not love you-- prayer's ineffectual see.

Anytime you're praying on him from desperation he's preying on you being obviously weakened.

Feeling like she can make a man love her indicates low self-esteem and it's opposite to a queen.

A woman wizened by life waits for a man to lead. He must prove his intentions lest a heart bleed.

If he proves/articulates his affections she can approve but to make him love her is just plain crude.

She prays five, ten, fifteen years and she's still not loved yet, not the way she deserves and wants.

BECOME FIRST, THEN CHOOSE SIRS

She BECOMES who she's supposed to be, her destiny--and THEN attracts men and chooses rightly.

The unenlightened man may not love her but loves having sex as a biological need whenever.

She serves a biological function and that's not lovin'. He does not love her but she'll be prayin'.

BETRAYAL TRAUMA

Using sex to bring love disintegrates the woman emotionally as increasingly she's treated badly.

She uses sex with a man to buffer loneliness but ends up far, FAR lonelier because she had sex.

BROKEN: PEARLS BEFORE SWINE

Her broken consciousness allows her casting pearls before swine but is trampled by em, aye.

She gave her greatest value away for nothing to one who didn't even deserve a conversation.

Afterwards she's left by herself in her house to ponder the massive mistake she just made in hell.

Living in a debauched Dionysian generation it's hard to tell where a line is for most of you silly gals.

The man has not honored you as his wife Miss, yet a roll in the hay will remedy your loneliness?

Your default setting must be chastity not "maybe". Get hep about this or be in the dumps quickly.

MALE RESPECT FOR A WOMAN

I've never seen such a day when male disrespect for women has been so high. R C. Blakes

Disrespect of women for themselves has never been so high and men talk about it day and night.

The disrespect is so blatant men act like they don't even like women. We've never seen such contempt.

Gov Ed is cancerous pop culture. I sensed it in the seventies but now it's gone way out there.

BETRAYAL TRAUMA

The left owns the five megaphones: media, entertainment, academia, science and medicine.

ANTI-WOMAN HATRED

Why anti-women hatred/contempt by men? Male respect comes from revelation of her value.

Regarding her value: The biggest complaint of women is the childish perspectives of men: SMV.

When he lacks ability to discern the true divine value of a woman in his life he disrespects her, aye.

He disrespects if he doesn't see his divine role in her life as well. One is heavenly, the other low level.

A little man wrecking women is a child. He's working games, his game is looks, he's running wild.

Little boys don't know there are limits when dealing with girls. LIttle men fight with women [ogres].

Men in their fifties and sixties intentionally hurting women cuz the little boy stayed the same.

He thought as a child but when he became a man he put away childish things. Fighting girls see.

GENERATION OF ARRESTED DEVELOPMENT

Recall we have a generation of men suffering from arrested development--don't forget that.

As childish as any little boy running around the school yard--yet he has a man's body and beard.

Childish boys fight with little girls because they haven't become grown men yet/still immature.

BETRAYAL TRAUMA

Any man who intentionally disrespects woman is a child: arrested development, little boys, defiled.

LITTLE BOYS HUMILIATE GIRLS

Little boys humiliate and hurt little girls. And it's the same when an old man hurts a 40 year old.

Little boys have not established understanding of the differences between male and female.

A mature man sees men are stronger. No fights, trying to break a woman down and still hurt her .

There's nothing more valuable to a heterosexual man than a woman. Without her he feels nothing.

Women are godly gifts to a man sir. This explains why happily married men live ten years longer.

Once a man matures he understands the devastating impact his words have on a woman: sad.

A masculine man chooses words very carefully cuz the last thing he wants to do is hurt her feelings.

He understands how his opinions/words effect her greatly and he is cognizant of this constantly.

MANHOOD USES CAREFUL WORDS

It's his manhood making him careful of his wife's tender feelings--more careful than anyone else see.

His opinions matter to her. He's careful all the time knowing the possible devastation or words.

With this kind of power over her he could create a wound that would never heal in the future.

BETRAYAL TRAUMA

A so-called masculine man disregarding the impact of his words on a woman? It's suspect/he's vermin.

He will weaponize her desire to please him. Its insatiable while he lords it over: bedlam.

A generation of men constantly breaking women cuz God has put within em desire to please HIM.

WEAPONIZING THE DESIRE TO PLEASE

When he's disrespectful he chips away at her self-perspective: inch by inch he does this.

A man seeing value knows women are agents of reproduction--multiplying whatever man gives em.

Full of seed but without a womb: filled with potential that will never manifest without a woman.

Right woman gives birth to a man's full potential. Like a child's toy that needs assembly, it's her call.

A disrespectful man can easily fracture and break the very woman ordained to be his helpmate.

A man can easily destroy his own future by destroying the woman ordained to be his partner.

A man struggling with self-hatred wrecks the self-esteem of a devoted woman and it's bad fated.

Way out in the wilderness I was always imposed on by uninvited guests so now I have a fence.

Having to adapt to them was like being hit with rocks and I wanted only to escape--this sux!

SELF-HATRED OF MALE ABUSERS

BETRAYAL TRAUMA

Men who flippantly and blatantly disrespect women are showing self-hatred and are not real men.

Love your wives as your own bodies. A man hating a woman hates his own flesh, what a pity.

The man should nourish and cherish her as he does the church. To love the woman is natural sarge.

A man hating a woman is self-hating for he's supposed to take care of women, always overlooking.

An alpha males says "I deal with her very carefully, very respectfully". He never curses her out see.

An alpha male's wife never fears he's about to get physical. A fruit of the spirit is self-control.

She can be flip but to the extent he loves himself he loves his woman who he always respects.

REVELATION OF WOMAN'S VALUE

A man separates himself before disrespecting a woman since it reflects on his self-perspective son.

In this women-hating generation a man will have to get a REVELATION of her anointed value to him.

He's gotta get the pimp stuff outa his mind, the garbage he learned at the barber shop or online.

The revelation is the non-sexual value of a woman and a man's purpose in her life in God's kingdom.

He must renew his mind from misogynistic propaganda: the more sex he had the more man, yah.

When alone I was a target for men: the hate hurt deeply but when married this stopped suddenly.

BETRAYAL TRAUMA

Being condemned without judge nor jury cuz they heard something and tucked it away until today.

The local pastors protected me and their loving respect for ladies saved me like a spiritual father see.

Taught by the old dons the more women they slept with the ore man they were, so many it's a blur.

TAUGHT BY MALE HATE

I thank God daily I'm protected behind a locked gate because I have experienced male hate.

When hubs picked up drink again he hated me suddenly, whereas before we were extremely happy.

Men hate, women chime in. Women hate, needing men is the only solution since kindergarten.

Calling women "B's" and "Hoes" and the women call themselves that while taking all their crap.

Misogyny, or the ingrained prejudice against women, has trained men how to behave like vermin.

Antiquated or false churches propound a message of misogyny by taking a bad man's side see.

The bible is twisted to make the man superior to the woman because he's a man, which is false.

NASTY MALE CULTURE

A well adjusted hetero man is not fighting with women. A meanie has gone awry in sex frustration.

He's had pimps for his mentors and other poor examples of manhood like evil barbers in all cultures.

BETRAYAL TRAUMA

He's bitter from a previous rejection. Heartbroken by a woman in the past, every woman pays son.

Any well adjusted masculine man loves womanhood too much to intentionally injure/cause a fuss.

For the woman is the GLORY of the man. For man is not of woman but woman of the man.

A true leader has the strength not to fall in with the mass, to do things his way nevertheless.

God's kings don't listen to Tik Tok or the barbershop about women they have their own mind man.

"You see a woman you'd love to hit on but don't tell your woman" said barber to innocent young man.

I'm not gonna pick a fight with him cuz I know he's mean and down putting so I just walk away gently.

ANTI-WOMAN BIAS

The anti-woman bias and downright hate is palpable to any woman no longer broken/aware of it all.

He says he wants only positivity but is nasty to anyone disagreeing or seeing things differently.

Having to adapt to some fool became an open wound as I lived in the land of the dumb called "cool".

The anti-woman bias of both sexes is palpable. This is very relieving, taking it out of the personal.

They endanger women by not doing what they should: protecting them from molestation.

When he returned to drink he stopped protecting wife and threw her to the wolves and strife.

BETRAYAL TRAUMA

MOTHER WOUNDS SET THE STAGE

Men hate women for many reasons in this misogynistic propaganda, this woman-hating rhetoric.

Society trains men to hate women cuz they already had a mother wound they never recovered from.

Mother wounds set the stage for incomprehensible abuse of women--getting back at mom.

Mom did something--take his pet away or be with men in the hay--and he's getting back every day.

Watch your pets when with immature men cuz someone did that to them: destroy a beloved friend.

To have my happy loving menagerie I had to relocate see cuz pets were destroyed by frenemies.

Kübler-Ross saw the connection between loss of pets in childhood as linked to abuse and psychosis.

That's how immature mom gets back at him or controls him: threatening to remove his furry friend.

ABUSE VICTIM BEHAVIORS

Culture man has a frustrated sexuality. That's why he's fighting with women and disrespecting see.

Women get back at men for this by becoming promiscuous but this never works miss.

Signs of mental abuse: always apologizing, fight-flight, exaggerated startle reflex, wrecked.

After living in fight flight survival mode tiny things sting and they need constant reassurance see.

BETRAYAL TRAUMA

Their perceptions have been warped so they need to know: do I look good enough, do I show well?

The abuse victim must test reality constantly: Am I seeing correctly, what is happening to me?

After having all aspects of self belittled or criticized they don't believe there's any good--downsized.

As victim the punishment never fit the crime so just a raised voice triggers recall of bad times.

The abuse victim may be extremely prickly around authority even if that voice is raised slightly.

VICTIMS AND BOUNDARIES

The victim is shocked when anyone's nice, they don't feel worthy of any gifts or helpful advice.

After being teased, taunted, humiliated and degraded the victim can't make decisions effective.

Anger/frustration comes easily to the abused see, then they're the ones accused of treachery.

Trauma shows up in our REACTIONS and sometimes they can look intense, criminal at times.

When hyper-stressed the victim can't access the logical so the reactions seem way unproportional.

Constantly defending themselves/accused tho' false they're timid and dubious of their talents.

Victims of longterm abuse develop Stockholm Syndrome, even loving the mean abuser too.

Her beta male allowed her to go off deep end--she was compelled to test him up to until rejection.

BETRAYAL TRAUMA

Her beta male allowed her to go off a cliff until she went so crazy he rejected the witch/that was it.

Mom created a monster by never correcting her but instead insulting her in front of others.

SILLY WOMEN WITHOUT WISDOM

Wicked men creep into houses and lead captive silly women laden with sins/driven by lusts.

You can't be a silly woman in a sick world. It's too easy for wicked men to run game on you girls.

A silly girl without wisdom is eaten alive as this world will expose her and ridicule her to the tribe.

There are too many women uneducated about manipulators ready to use em {not just neglected}.

Silly women have no mind of their own, they're complete conformists to the other women [dumbed].

Women are always reading books but can't come to knowledge of the truth-- they're being used.

A silly woman entertains men that creep. They creep into her house and she entertains em see.

Creepy men defined: they're unstable, uncommitted, living their lives loosely-- and silly women like!

Why do so many men sleep around so much? Because so many women let them. R. C. Blakes

I'm speaking woman to women. I've been around and this info will save your lives from a dungeon.

This is all vital info your daddy shoulda taught you BEFORE he released you to the world.

BETRAYAL TRAUMA

DON'T ENTERTAIN CREEPS IN YOUR HOUSE

Entertaining men who creep into your house shows immaturity and lack of judgement: ouch.

JUST BECAUSE he comes to the door [never announcing himself before] you let him in?

Why does she have such poor judgement? That she would allow a man to creep into her space?

When someone's in your house you gotta adapt to their words, personality, attitudes—no way/ouch!

Women have become silly, gullible and loose, entertaining wicked men who are similar too.

Why is he coming to your house unannounced? Do you have good herb, is he crashing your dinner?

A silly woman feels she has to have a man to have value because the world taught her that too.

Why is he coming to your house unannounced? Do you have good herb, is he coming for lunch?

You do great, interesting & fun things and he wants some too. You're not entertainment: eschew.

The world has incarcerated women to no appreciation of self without a man, like avoiding hell.

As a result women may settle for a piece of a man not a whole one for being alone they can't fathom.

WOMEN FERTILIZE MALE DISRESPECT

Modern females have fertilized disrespect of a generation of men, by how they dress/talk etc.

BETRAYAL TRAUMA

He may have entered in with a respectful mindset but the way she acted quickly degraded that.

A virtuous woman manages her life with judgement, discretion, boundaries and self-respect.

A queen of a woman will allow her heart to be crushed before she allows any disrespect as such.

She will pack her bags and get moving before she settles for disrespect from men [dull/boring].

A tsunami of male disrespect is planted in the way women disrespect themselves, ya think?

A high standard is ultimate feminine energy to attract a husband but the world says it doesn't.

Taking on society's low standards, a woman removes the main thing attracting a good husband.

A good man wants a virtuous woman who manages herself with certain standards, no?

WOMEN FERTILIZE MISOGONY

If she disrespects herself she fertilizes the engine of misogyny and the culture wants that see.

She who commands respect from man is the one who lives her life with excellence and limits.

The queen is a woman who provides consequences for any disrespect and that's why she gets it.

If there are no consequences for bad behavior there will be no respect as things get worse in fact.

A woman who accepts bad behavior without consequences does not love herself sis.

BETRAYAL TRAUMA

With self-disrespect the world takes you far beyond where you prefer to go, down a rabbit hole.

HONOR MEN WHO HONOR YOU

The woman must honor man for respecting her by reciprocating and that keeps sweetness going.

In many cases the more he's respectful the more the woman becomes dishonorable: unbelievable.

Women are conditioned to male imagery but reject male character due to broken consciousness sir.

Broken consciousness makes a respectful man unattractive. She's turned off by niceness.

A respectful man is rarely appreciated by women while male disrespect is pursued with a passion.

Many women have turned a good man bad, as they did not honor their man's respect: how sad.

When women don't honor male respect they are training a new generation of men who abuse: sick.

A good wife prefers him with loving concern, treasuring and honoring him while holding him dear.

A good wife sees to it that she respects and delights in her husband: she notices/prefers him.

Silly women let men creep into their intimate space. This shows their lack of boundaries ok.

Allowing creeping invasions goes along with overextending financially when asked of them.

Being used for shelter or money goes along with allowing men to use them sexually.

BETRAYAL TRAUMA

Letting a man into her intimate space is even worse if she's a mother with children, it complicates.

So desperate for a man she lets em in on her children's space and jeopardizes them seriously ok.

She wants a man so bad she lets em abuse her kids. She's a mother but having a man is first.

Say: "I don't see things that way and I don't have to sit here being insulted by you": no more blues.

MORE ABOUT CREEPING MEN

You're a mother. You don't have a right to allow men to go creeping in and out your house ever.

Come on woman: he creeps in for a bootie call then you don't see him again for weeks--get wisdom.

Every time he calls with his jive talk you fall for it again and it's been going on for years woman.

I see extremely intelligent/spiritual women being made fools of unnecessarily and it's scary.

Love with intelligence not maudlin mush and gush. Don't lose yourself in this temporary rush.

Not only do they entertain/allow men to creep into their houses, they are then led into bondage.

How much can a man damage your life and rob you before you wake up and say "no more"?

SILLY WOMEN GIVE IN

After his postorgasmic rejection she vows never to see him again then he calls and she caves in.

BETRAYAL TRAUMA

He says "I don't understand" so she tries to explain and before you know it she's back in his cage.

A moral woman would slap/shut the door in his face but she futilely tries to explain the disgrace.

MOVE ON, MOVE ON

He's given her STDs, her credit is ruined and she's lost her reputation--maybe she should move on.

Instead of moving on from this wicked guy immediately you allowed him to lead you captive lady.

When a woman finds the right man/the right leader submission will come automatically sir.

When she finds the right man she'll submit naturally but until then it's ok to be feisty and testy.

How a woman can spend her life following clowns! She feels less vulnerable if he's down.

CLOWNS LEAVE WOUNDS

The clowns leave such a wound in her life she's a bitter rage-aholic when her king shows up, aye.

She's become so calloused she won't follow the king. She's too warped to submit naturally.

You must VET the man. If he's not proven himself thru knowledge and character he doesn't get in.

If you allow clowns into your house to lead you you are a silly woman going right into judgment/ruin.

A silly woman follows men who are going nowhere. Just cuz you need a man/little boy with beard.

BETRAYAL TRAUMA

She "needs" a man. She's out of control sexually as her passions trigger this common tragedy.

Her passions have overridden her intelligence and shut off her spiritual discernment of disgust.

CHASTITY BRINGS DISCERNMENT

As chastity is gone so is discernment as millions of queens are led by fools every moment.

She doesn't want to hear this at first when he's creeping in & out of her house just after her loss.

Only when that fool leads her into captivity and bondage with her life broken will she listen.

When the fool walks away now she seeks advice: that's how all-consuming/addicting sex is, aye.

She's a silly woman cuz she knows too much/too intelligent for this yet opens her door to twits.

The captive woman ignores the Holy Spirit and has shut off her brain, her perceptions defective ok.

A silly woman is driven by pure passion and lust. Men aren't the only sex addicts/there's no disgust.

The silly woman allows the fool to lead her into bondage and the silly man an ignoramus.

An ignoramus, a dummy, an airhead: that's who leads a man into bondage--be chaste instead.

A man who can make many babies but can't raise children. He can have sex but isn't lovin'.

He can do what any cow, dog, goat or cat can do and you're impressed with a big dummy too.

BETRAYAL TRAUMA

SEEK MEN WHO RESPECT VALUE

You want not only a man who's knowledgeable but one who discerns and respects your value.

You don't have to beg him to see who you are, he knows it, that's why it's so easy to submit dear.

He's not honoring you creeping into your house to have sex while the kids are sleeping/he's a louse.

You don't need a man creeping in for sex and two minutes after he can't wait to go/he exits.

He wants nothing but sex from her--he's creeping. He knows nothing but it's ok, she's accepting.

"All men are dogs" but they wouldn't be that way if women would take the reins as they say.

I pray every shackle and psychological block be broken off of you now. As it is in heaven, so below.

NARCISSISTS AND DISREGULATION

Longterm damage from the narcissist: emotional scarring/open wounds after being humiliated.

Mental/emotional anguish from being shamed: all they do is sit red-faced wishing the pain away.

The pain never goes away cuz it's the natural byproduct of you being with that narcissist ok.

Emotional confusion results from being the recipient of narcissistic anger: it infiltrates the mind sir.

A narc's anger stings, it hurts leaving a bitter aftertaste and on other relationships, a curse.

BETRAYAL TRAUMA

Now am I not only misunderstood I am ridiculed for feeling as I do, for looks destroyed too.

LONGTERM CONSEQUENCES OF BEING HATED

After being told repeatedly how pitiable you are it erodes your interior, it's inevitable sir.

How the pain remains: you've been alienated from potentially vibrant or rewarding friends.

Being on the receiving end of hatred and contempt leaves a body wrecked as friends exit.

After his sting-shot her looks were destroyed in a self-esteem leak so he ridiculed her again see.

The worst thing you do is take advice from a narcissist as he puts your way down and implants his.

He says you want everything your own way: You work your fingers to the bone while he sits ok.

With self-awareness even one sentence becomes a red flag and it's shocking, alarming, disclosing.

But with denseness these sting shots are like bats in the night constantly cutting her down to size.

HE'S JUST A DIRTY OLD MAN

He's just a dirty old man. There's no fool like an old fool and it's embarrassing to the clan.

Great changes occur when aware of pervasive woman-hate affecting every female on the planet.

Could you leave the sarcasm behind Satan? I feel bruised just cuz I'm sitting next to you.

BETRAYAL TRAUMA

I don't know the creep/I don't care. I dust my hands off, no more charades, I never took the lure.

Abuse. I wasn't in a war/prison just a small liberal town with no privacy/solitude as I planned.

You talk about mobbings, gang-ups and pack murders. This was strenuous/put me in constant fear.

I'm sorry to reveal all the pain caused by psychopaths but it all brings growth--see it as positive.

EXPERIENCE MAKES YOU RELATABLE

Now that you've experienced this you're relatable to all the millions abused by modern narcissists.

You can't change outer circumstance--he's obdurate--so you change self, adorable/cute as hell.

Get out Satan. I don't know you/never knew you and don't want to, I've learned all I'm supposed to.

There's gotta be consequences for bad behavior or its fertilizing a generation of female haters.

Use these experiences towards empathy for others for its in the billions in these days/the latter.

Like when you were stupid and naive enough to go live with a man who turned against you then.

TRAUMA BONDING WITH NARCISSISTS

To the trauma bonded: you're with a pathological person who is disturbed--beware/watch out.

The person who's trauma bonded is very self-limited, is exhausted, feels unworthy of all but the pits.

BETRAYAL TRAUMA

As the victim weakens daily the perpetrator becomes more diabolical because to him its like a pill.

It's diabolical, of the devil, truly evil when one makes the other know who's in charge and to be still.

Grind you to the ground: you're to have little belief in yourself as they wish to fill you with them.

They demand your total subjugation and over time to avoid serious wrath you become a yes person.

SHAMING INTO A YES PERSON

After constant shaming I finally asked myself: Who am I and how the hell did I get here? Survivor

My worth & self-respect weren't just stolen they were trampled upon. I have doubts, a ton. Survivor

Another: "I feel like damaged goods. Will I ever be acceptable again? I'm obsolete/done in."

He came at me with his imperative thinking: you must, you should. It was a very hard life and cold.

It is necessary to declare your freedom. You get to choose for yourself tho' you feel imprisoned.

Defending yourself beyond necessary, over-explaining to everybody: these are the effects today.

The narcissist has strong opinions and there no adjustments so say no or stay stuck with him.

A puppet is not living, it's being managed. Average women are controlled by remote sources.

Average women controlled by a sisterhood they don't wanna disappoint, that's their weak point.

BETRAYAL TRAUMA

There are average men controlled by a toxic brotherhood, it's subliminal just getting a haircut.

The world will pull the puppet strings but won't deal with the consequences: destroying queens.

Cutting puppet strings means finally living your life authentically and that is true maturity.

APPROVAL OF AN INFERIOR CIRCLE

Stop living for people's approval and you're on your way to selfhood and separation from evil.

To end self-sabotage you must own your personal vision and stop shrinking for approval getting.

You stop being who you are--pursuing vision--to satisfy an inferior circle who don't deserve you.

Separation anxiety takes over. But elevation always calls for separation, it's the only answer.

You can't win the race while running with the pack. It's homeostasis--they'll always hold you back.

TO WIN THE RACE, SEPARATE

If you wanna win the race separate from the pack. Your destiny is entirely unique, peculiar in fact.

Self-sabotage comes from not owning your personal vision. You're bigger than those around.

You don't wanna own that vision for fear of how they'll react or if truth be known, walking alone.

If you can't walk alone you can't win. It's scary, no friends, but then turn to God, amen.

BETRAYAL TRAUMA

When you're up all night working fingers to the bone that's your vision with you on the throne.

Frenemies detect withdrawn attention due to that very vision and will surely be an obstruction.

Problems came from people in your life. Either letting em in or not withdrawing with strife.

You let ruffians in your house then are amazed at the destruction from their toot and raucous.

THE BEST CHOOSES THE WORST

The best of men are choosing the worst of women and the best of women the worst of men.

The world says: "this is what you want". So good men and women bypass the best for grunts.

Men are going for women who aren't wife material, without the mindset of a spouse at all.

A woman can't choose a man who's too small for her. Words have a spiritual impact, triggers.

Choose: words can impact how you think, feel and move. Language can break the soul too.

Go with vision, cut strings, watch language and choose rightly. Now you gotta watch his energy.

His energy is the atmosphere he creates around you and your spirit is sensitive to this energy too.

When energy doesn't feel right that's God saying to you: RUN, get the hell out/don't look back too.

It doesn't matter how good he looks, you're about to sabotage your life forever with this kook.

BETRAYAL TRAUMA

There's an anti-woman bias to begin with and you're trusting Mr. Flashy who's psychopathic?

There's a woman-hating bias with most men so you must carefully find/choose that good one.

DEMONIC ENERGY IGNORED

You're looking at his height or pics on instagram not his horns or the demonic energy of this goon.

Wrong energy will always disturb your spirit. The wrong person is thusly sabotaging your environment.

There's a spirit in man and inspiration of the almighty giveth them understanding. Job 32: 8.

It doesn't matter what he says/how helpful he was--the spirit in him felt unsettling and vicious.

Rather than dealing with a vicious spirit who ghosts you just cut your losses and run/escape Sue.

The most vicious spirits can look good/be nice but Lucifer is like that: brilliant, shining bright.

These people are dangerous. Many are killed by close relationships so avoid mindless twits.

LOST CONNECTION TO THE SELF

You're better than any you're attracted to. Recall we're born whole then mal-adapt to scrooge.

We lost connection to the true self which is divinely made in His image—as reflected in our mates.

Broken consciousness chooses weird mates. Either as social connects or painful opposites.

BETRAYAL TRAUMA

Instead of praying he'll love you just know he is not your husband, dust off your hands and move on.

When devil is the default setting anything can happen and everything did so now self-forgive.

You know what you have for the world so shake off this inherited shame keeping you in a whirl.

Inherited shame: past relics impose on the present and wreck/break consciousness every day.

FALSE FEMALE FRIENDS

A queen doesn't compete with any other woman. Dust off hands/move on to superior position.

A troublemaker plants seeds of strife and gossip separates the best of friends. Prov. 16: 28

Watch out if they can't be happy for you. Jealousy is deep within them so set boundaries too.

Gossip is not something you want in any of your friendships. Go grey rock when you detect it.

They constantly copy and one-up you. The minute they get a leg up they take over completely too.

The copiers are dangerous since it indicates envy. Leave em alone so they can grow see.

They must grow confident in who God created them to be, not always copying thee. Get free.

Competition brings out greed and avarice at its worst. Terrible things can happen like divorce.

Frenemies align with you publicly but bash you privately. Other people like you so they use that see.

BETRAYAL TRAUMA

You're a trophy friend but they really don't like you and would quickly ditch you if you failed too.

Trophy friends are always gossiped about. You want real friends who honor you in private.

DISTANCE, BOUNDARIES, CONVERSATION

See a problem and you may have to distance yourself, set boundaries or have a conversation.

You're always there for them but they often flake out too. It's a one-sided relationship/skewed.

If it's one-sided they may be using you so learn what your needs are, refuse to be conquered.

They need your services but don't wanna pay so align as your friend so you answer questions ok.

They use you for your gifts, time, talents and help and that's the only time they connect, hell!

They're not your friend, they're using you to get stuff done so don't feel flattered just wall in.

Are you a friend or client? Are you a true friend of mine or are you ready to pay for my time?

FRIEND OR CLIENT?

They use you for what you do but will not invest in you as a person/get to know you better too.

Do they see you as mentor? Your clay feet brings a spirit of familiarity and resentment in future.

They refuse to open up to you, everything is surface or nonpersonal and then reject you if you do.

BETRAYAL TRAUMA

They aren't a friend if they judge you. You know they're judging you cuz they ghost you too.

You confide in them as friends and they ghost you in judgment in return: go grey rock, discern.

There are some who come in and out of your life. The first couple times it hurts until you realize.

Playing games with relationships is something you must not do lest you wanna be alone/blue.

Rather than pay for services they become a frenemy to get stuff done then waste your time see.

BECOME EMOTIONALLY IMPERVIOUS

Become warm but emotionally impervious to these ruptures that would hurt any other.

Become so emotionally self-sufficient you're prepared for people coming in/suddenly going out.

Imagine a warzone where suddenly people are gone and there is no relational predictability.

The only healthy adaptation is aristocratic reserve: hold your head up high and just be of service.

Like any warzone each time you see em may be your last so why play games with relationships lass?

Guard your heart. If your needs are predictability then get distance from the gossip, ghoster, tart.

The most important red flag is not what you see but what you feel—now you can avoid trouble.

When one is unhealthy for your life there's an energy you feel/should pay attention to now.

BETRAYAL TRAUMA

When you let a man mistreat you then your personal standard is re-set--good luck with that.

The most important priority is peace. If he causes you anxiety he's gotta go cuz it's prioritized see.

TRAPPED AND GOING NOWHERE

Trapped in relationships going nowhere: it's clear to you too but you can't see the GREAT danger.

It has been a waste of your life and a waste of time. How many years have been consumed? Aye

How did it get started? Love bombing. He steered you through extreme attention and affection.

"Thru flattery she forced him" the bible says: she overwhelmed him, a lamb to the slaughter.

Lovebombing the trauma bonded is easy. This is a lesson that school boys learn early.

They learn in the locker room that a girl without a daddy is easy and all you gotta do is woo her see.

LOVE STARVED WOMEN FALL IN

After being in a situation without love and affection this new guy lovebombs her and she lays down.

How would you know the difference? You never had true attention, affection or authenticity sis.

How would you know this was fake, a manipulation for supply, a trap to set you up/tie your soul up?

Once implanting their stinger they could manipulate and control you from the inside out: no more.

BETRAYAL TRAUMA

Suddenly they're blowing your phone up with texts everywhere and you're enmeshed in a snare.

Suddenly there are hearts over the screen & I love yous written here and there so surely he cares.

They're at your house soon as you arrive. They're loveboming after being starved for love, aye.

It's like a giant wave that picks you up and carries you away. You're so starved for attention its ok.

A man that flattereth his neighbor sets a net for his feet, making his victim fall cuz he can't move see.

LOVE BOMBING TO BRING A FALL

Fall: Loveboming is designed to make the victim FALL in love instead of intentionally walking in love.

Love Bombing gets you so carried away emotionally you have no time to think then you're trapped see.

It all happened so fast you just go caught up and before you knew it you fell in love with the devil.

They smother you, giving you no time to think. They solve problem/take your side on everything.

They just lovin' on you and you know something's wrong but it all seems so right all day and night.

Gee I always prayed for someone to love me like this but it just doesn't feel authentic some way sis.

Just when she sees it may be a scam here comes another dozen roses and she's weakening.

The manipulated love smitten doesn't realize the person is setting him up for emotional maelstrom.

BETRAYAL TRAUMA

Does she ever think: This is not real/not authentic and it's not gonna last? No, she's having a blast.

Wicked create obstacles & dissension but mostly they introduce temptations to trap you son.

They tempt you with things contrary to how you've learned. Turn away, they're not of Christ.

Deviation from a topic mid-sentence is a sign of dementia, cognitive decline or a gotcha.

They were strong, ambitious & talked about grownup things but now they're malicious & useless see.

GOD RESCUES US FROM TOXICITY

God rescues you from toxicity into safety so your complaint of the past is an insult honey.

Disrespect is shown by pressuring you to do things that you don't want to do. Nip it in the bud Sue.

"NO" is a complete sentence. If someone keeps pressuring you call em out-- it's disrespect.

By smooth and flattering speech they deceive the hearts of the unsuspecting: innocent/naive.

A wizened person is not affected by love bombing in fact it's a presumptuous turnoff & irritation.

They're smothering you, it's all good but there's something not right about it in the spiritual.

Love bombing happens to men too. There's a new generation of women the clever shrews.

Women are clever love bombers and once they got him locked in the game changes again hon'

BETRAYAL TRAUMA

These guys will blow your mind and they know all the tricks until you're locked in that box.

Once committed the roses stop, the calls are lessened and there is an avoidance of intimacy.

Now you realize he started with dessert: lotsa sugar, no nourishment and intimacy is a dearth.

EMOTIONAL UNAVAILABILITY

They move from love bombing to emotional unavailability which is a hurt and shock honey.

They'll gladly give you access to their body but never their soul or heart. It's a cold environment.

A man makes a woman's body respond physically but does nothing for her mind, nothing at all honey.

Addict you to the love bombing and when you require more than flattery they leave you hanging.

He can lovebomb you all the way to the altar and you wake up the next day to a shallow monster.

"This guy has NO depth." That was the sad realization of one love bombed victim before she left.

You married a dam narcissist who just needed to marry someone for his own purposes sis.

Addict you to the love bombing then leave you hanging when you want more, to put it simply.

The lovebomb/withdraw cycle is like an itch she can't scratch and I was there once/it's a bitch.

There's something missing, she don't know what. He knows how to have sex but not to make love.

BETRAYAL TRAUMA

Any woman with early trauma gets sucked in very easily--please teach her decency & boundaries.

He knows how to make her body respond to lock her in but never has love for her as in covenant.

He knows how to have sex [like all animals] but cannot conversate, he's disconnected totally ok.

BLINDED BY SEX AND ROMANCE

The lovestarved female is so taken away by romance and sex she can't see his low shallowness.

So taken in by sexual prowess she can't see his apathy to her conversation or personality.

He hasn't said two words nor has he responded to her for years and she wonders why life hurts.

He's so full of ego he's empty of soul and real personality and that's the end of it sweetie.

You're deep and full of emotion, he's shallow and emotionally brittle and that's the end/all.

Who you are internally, spiritually, emotionally: he couldn't care less about this stuff see.

Let alone intellectually: this guy does not relate to you, has nothing in common with you, a dud see.

NO CONNECTEDNESS

They will not engage in heart conversations. They have to go to work, they find any excuse to shirk.

They will give you a cookie cutter answer then slide on out of it. They will not discuss girl stuff.

BETRAYAL TRAUMA

When she says how much she's hurting he can't provide any empathy since he's avoiding intimacy.

Avoiding intimacy rules: they can't feel your pain and won't have a response to your truth.

Most importantly, they won't have an interest in your goals. You've felt that from long ago.

You can be so excited discussing your plans and they'll give lip service changing the subject fast.

This disconnectedness from everything above will cause frustration in you or degradation to a shrew.

SHALLOW CONVERSATION

They're uncomfortable in silence. They break it with small talk, turn the radio on, aggravate us.

They cannot be in silence cuz they cannot connect to you intimately: it's all surface personality.

These are the things which must be discovered before going too far: go deep before you leap.

Questions: Does this person desire to be intimate with me, does he even have the rare capacity?

Youth with depth assume others have it too but sagacious elder knows we're not one but two.

Sex is not intimacy. Intimacy goes deeper than the love bombing surface stuff and it's consistent.

True love is deep and consistent. Consistency is the greatest gift a man can give his woman.

The third trap is gaslighting. Abuse you emotionally then make you believe it's your imagining.

BETRAYAL TRAUMA

What you know is just common sense they will make you doubt till you can't trust your thoughts.

TO WALK OUT FIRST WAKE UP

To walk out you must first wake up by asking: what exactly are you getting from straw-grabbing?

You say you love that person so much but exactly are you getting from that lascivious lug?

A relationship is supposed to go both ways. Compare your deposits vs what's been taken away.

The foundation: was God in it? If God was in it you'd not be separated from morals, family, money.

Sometimes the hardest thing to face is truth. Truth is never your enabler but your best friend too.

The truth slaps us around a bit but we're always better for it. He's not into you/using you, leave quick.

So you were belittled and discarded. You weren't put in a concentration camp or murdered.

I rescued you from that so why you complaining about it? I gave you a castle/you're free of the rat.

HEART GOTTA BREAK TO HEAL

Sometimes a heart gotta break for a soul to heal. Look around--is THIS what you're supposed to be?

Am I supposed to be depleted all the time and crying? Before you walk out wake up to his lying.

Wake up first, activate your will second. It's been kept quiet and still being shut up and hog bound.

BETRAYAL TRAUMA

He made a decision to go to another land & a decision to get out and back: It's the WILL not lack.

If she doesn't make a decision and activate her will against this sick thing she's doomed see.

Doomed: you give time & dedication to a clown who never deserved a conversation/years gone.

Activate your will and decide to end it. Otherwise you'll get old telling youth why and how to avoid it.

If you haven't activated a will to get out stop sending me ten page letters describing the lout.

Nothing I can tell you changes your situation until you activate your will--that's the bottom line girl.

INSANE LOVE IS TRAUMA BOND

The intensity of the "love" you feel is just a trauma bond, a tsunami of terror starting in the womb.

You gotta look yourself in the mirror and say "I'm done" then waste no time getting the hell outa town.

When you finally activate your will you'll tell nobody. You'll just move forward to new life finally.

An activated will turns into momentum and action. It gets the ball rolling and your faith gives traction.

Before I did a lot of talk convincing no one, now I silently move into destiny far away from you hon'.

The Lord said He set life and death before us--the choice is ours. A soul tie is death/horrors.

Sometimes the only way to victory is to outlive the enemy: when they die there is no memory.

BETRAYAL TRAUMA

DYSFUNCTIONAL FAMILIARITY

You gotta leave the dysfunctional familiarity. This toxic connection we call a trauma bond see.

The dysfunctional familiarity is all she's known but God will now receive her so she's never alone.

The holy spirit only moves in when she's finally dismissed the others in this sick system.

The way you dismiss others is to give them the gift of your absence then God gives you guidance.

Where's it going if you don't leave this situation? Despite toxic nostalgia death is the outcome.

Biblical repentance is not just being sorry but changing the direction of your walk and getting out.

REPENTANCE = BACK TO GOD'S GRACE

Repentance puts you back in a place of God's grace, not being sorry but not changing your pace.

If you're not ready to leave you've not repented yet since direction of the walk determines it.

Keep going until you kill it. Keep going in that direction when the flesh calls you back and mean it.

It's hard. You'll have days when toxic nostalgia will call you back: let's give it another shot Jack.

You'll have days when he sends notes and flowers trying to trigger that soul tie: temple of horrors.

Keep going until you kill it. That soul tie is a living thing: demons that are suffocating your spirit.

BETRAYAL TRAUMA

Terror of the unknown takes over at this point but know God waits on the other side to anoint.

Prodigal son left a foreign country and kept going: you can't afford to have friends from that city.

Old friends may wanna remind you of that or keep pulling you into it: anchors to the pit.

When Lot was leaving Sodom and Gomorrah God said don't look back [don't give it life again].

Lot's wife had toxic nostalgia for the city and looked back--only to be turned into a pillar of salt.

MOVE AWAY FROM SOUL TIES

Moving away from soul tie badness is the only path. Once you finally see that it's over at last.

It's not an easy path but the only path. By moving away you deprive it of oxygen/avoid God's wrath.

While you put distance with a soul tie you suffocate it and it dies. Can you hold out while you cry?

Now you must simultaneously draw closer to God then He smoothens the rest of the way out.

Instead of suffocating more you allow God you revive you spiritually--you're euphoric, truly.

So as you leave you grow closer to God. Simultaneously you cleave: separate from friends/the mob.

Now you must feed your mind and soul with God's word, positive goals and healthy people.

FEED SOUL WITH GOD'S WORD

BETRAYAL TRAUMA

The further you get away from it the clearer you see how toxic and demonic it was & how dangerous.

As you move away from toxicity your mind is renewed and your true worth is back in tune.

Now your visions, hopes and dreams come alive again. They died, suffocated by whims of men.

Your beautiful dreams died while you were tied in a knot with a man who was rot/loved you not.

Mind, vision, hopes, dreams and plans are all renewed. Like dust off a mirror God makes you new.

All the beauty in your godly destiny comes alive again, you're returned from the dead/trash bin.

You may feel this situation robbed you of your life but you've got a whole lotta life to live son.

You feel this tie deprived you of all your worth and value, I did too--but they're innate, built in, true.

No devil in hell can touch your innate built-in value and it's instantly revived when God accepts you.

"When he came to himself": What he was returning to was self--for so long we missed the magic elf.

Stay alone for awhile to rekindle your relationship with two people: the Creator and your Self.

This is not the end of you. God has greater days ahead and it'll blow your mind what He has planned.

THOUGHTS OF THE DAY

The absence of bloat really makes a person stand out in the crowd. Imagine that, a cosmic joke so loud.

BETRAYAL TRAUMA

In fact that relation is so great they even call it Bulimic Shame and that's crucial to recovery ok.

Trauma-based edacity was so intense her eating disorder saved her from being a 600 pounder.

Some cats are very neurotic and if they are older it's obdurate so you just go along with it.

Every time you don't go to his page congratulate yourself ok for he's boring/you're the sage.

Glad-handing and back-slapping: that's the U.N. unity Biden's always talking about constantly.

Sanctioning means seizing assets so take Putin's yacht and do it now. Biden won't or he's so slow.

You've every right to Righteous Anger after being smeared by those aiming to hurt you sister.

Millions are awakening that it wasn't just rivalry it was sibling abuse and very malicious too.

RELATIONSHIP DESTRUCTION

The narcissist will stop at nothing to destroy and dismantle your relationships honey.

This is what they do, this is what they're good at. Great talents in manipulation & hicks politics.

Being emotional vampires they get off on tears and disrupting your affairs is supply for enviers.

Two sisters worked to destroy relationship with mom then she proceeded to triangulate with them.

It was the most frustrating situation I'd ever been in, the triangulations of three women envyin'.

BETRAYAL TRAUMA

Instead of facing blame of a mother they place that blame on someone else usually the younger.

TOXIC LEGACIES

A toxic legacy is a destructive pattern of painful and damaging behaviors handed down.

Its when one or more in a family system act in a very unhealthy, toxic and destructive manner.

Members will IMPRINT their own children with toxic words and actions and that's the system.

It is saddening to get the facts and stats on excruciating abuse within the home, hidden.

Intergenerational trauma significantly impacts the structure of each family and its robots.

Criticized, unloved, unworthy: it's how things are perceived that determines their story.

Trust is crushed in these systems and the children don't learn healthy boundaries: abuse recipe.

It's not that they have "trust issues" but that they were betrayed, crushed and damaged too.

The lethal family system has a code of silence while pretending everything's fine despite.

The abused child becomes withdrawn, quiet, shy and timid having been told he's irrelevant.

But as the child becomes an adult silence won't keep him safe anymore, he must fight this war.

Silence can steal your voice and take your life hostage in viscous abuse cycles lasting decades.

BETRAYAL TRAUMA

In fear you can't find your voice in the face of gaslighting, triangulation and blameshifting.

When children do speak out they're minimized: No, it's not true and naughty kid you're lying too.

CODEPENDENCY

Codependency is where one is dependent on another with a pathological condition: it happens.

They leave their mark like a scar tho' it's codependent relationships that are invisibly covert.

Sisters and mother dump ALL the shame and blame on the one scapegoat, that floats their boat.

Adverse childhood experiences [ACEs] are traumatic events changing the brain/causing stress.

ACEs cause devastating longterm problems like autoimmune diseases, cancer, heart, addictions.

BETRAYAL TRAUMA

Betrayal of innocent trust thru invalidation scars our core sense of who we are, it is destroyed.

It undermines self-confidence/esteem as well as belief system about the scary world we live in.

Because one's TRUST is shattered betrayal trauma is real and central to any study on this matter.

Ramifications of this setup are infinite. It's why one's a spender, gambler, sex addict, alcoholic.

A hurt is at the center of all addictions. It is present in all of them, all they do is to hold it all down.

BETRAYAL TRAUMA

Sadness, frustration and especially anger is part of the grief process and very necessary to it.

After trusting those people so much the betrayal trauma terrified me and made me sick in my gut.

LIGHT'S OUT, TERROR IN THE GUT

The terror went on for years, felt as homesickness or inadequacy. I was a weasel and queasily.

That terror felt in the gut was something catastrophic and I wanted to do anything to shut it up.

My world went topsy turvy in this circus and I was at the bottom again attracting more abusiveness.

I was so crushed/goals bashed/self trashed I became mousy, beholden, scared to death of em.

And it was lights out on the True Self, that was replaced with a neurotic get-along who was false.

Women who hate you, who are social & good at distorting truth, will make you sad and blue.

I knew she hated me so in my naiveté started gifting and she hated me even more, poor thing.

As to who is a superior man, toad to prince: it should be obvious but now we've missed this.

FLYING MONKEYS

Heartbreak of estrangement: breakdown of supportive relationships between family members.

Those who are supposed to support you, don't; on your side, aren't: you're left on your own.

BETRAYAL TRAUMA

You find real fast you're isolated and alone and must make important decisions about home.

The flying monkeys do the narcissist's bidding to inflict emotional/physical pain on the target.

Flying monkeys use gossip and they stoop quite low in the despicable things they say about the target.

They can't speak normally, it's all about retaliation and smear campaigns against that one.

The monkeys paint the narcissist as the victim. Here is more frustration as they run to console him.

They'll defend and protect the narcissist no matter what it involves or how much anyone resists.

They insist the problem is you since they are the majority but no, it's the opposite story.

Majority does not rule in psychology. They're a sick system stuck together without individuality.

The majority does not rule in truth. More often one man is a majority and the rest are stuck as fools.

Don't expect them to listen and behave, they'll deny everything and take their lies to the grave.

FEELING OF ZERO LOYALTY

It was the feeling of zero loyalty around me. Like I was the last person on earth deserving to be.

No wonder I freaked at six grade camp/church retreats: didn't wanna be so close to those creeps.

Going from a mal-adaptive home situation to week long retreats made me heartsick and freaked.

BETRAYAL TRAUMA

It's hard going up against the tyranny of the group but remember the majority is always untrue.

Monkeys are not loyal to you only malignant narcissist and they are vicious as a consequence.

I had no idea why Jezebel's friends were so nasty and mean to me. They were incited by her jealousy.

GET INTO YOUR OWN THING

A famous writer is both a product of his generation and a artistic survivor of the emotional trauma of it.

I do not think one can access a writer's motives without understanding his early development.

His subject matter's determined by the age in which he lives/an emotion from which he can't escape.

Before he even begins to write he's acquired an emotional attitude from which he can't escape.

Become an interesting person by not hankerin' over them but developing your own talents, and de-friend.

PEOPLE-WORSHIP

Think of all the minutes you wasted on them and don't waste one more. Now refocus on your own thing galore.

In twenty years no one will remember or give a care on top of it. We're only here for a minute, let go of it.

When empty/immature, we become how we're MIRRORED. I became exactly what accused of by sisters.

You can't stop taking credit or always thinking it's you. Ok but without a muse you'll run on empty soon.

BETRAYAL TRAUMA

I've blocked every channel so you can't reach me just cuz you want to anymore. I've had it/opened a new door.

Sorry, I can't let you determine my reality any longer. I won't be around so just say what you want.

The extreme emotional shock from my generation when intimately exposed to it I'll never forget.

It started in kindergarten when I had "school phobia"--I didn't wanna leave home and be around em.

I was so unhappy around peers I'd get stomach aches and crying jags. I sought older people as pals.

The next was high school '85 and my experience with them was a terrifying shock/something to despise.

I used alcohol as a social lubricant to adapt to those fools. I insulated myself from them all through school.

I feel SO much happier not letting curiosity kill the cat by going there, see? I feel exhilarated, happy, free.

The Big WAIT is over when the Potter say's He's done and you're perfect. I'm always ready/could be today.

WIVES OF PORN ADDICTS BECOME SUICIDAL

It's the wives of porn addicts who become suicidal. Connect to those who've experienced relational betrayal.

Living with a porn addict is coming to terms with betrayal trauma and it is now rampant in America.

The trauma of ongoing infidelity whether thru porn or affairs is so horrific as we lose our grips, it's tragic.

Relational betrayal thru porn is a very isolating experience as it means other lies like affairs or prostitutes.

BETRAYAL TRAUMA

It's a hellish ordeal to wake up to someone you thought you knew so well. It is a shock/trauma in lower hell.

It's a life of emotional manipulations and lying. Any woman smart/dumb knows something's up/debauchery.

What brings us to our knees is the cheating we discover, then the emotional manipulations so clever.

It's so tricky navigating thru the emotional manipulations increasingly hooked to his secret activities.

DARK NIGHT OF THE SOUL (I KNOW IT WELL)

It is sacred work helping women thru this dark night of the soul. It hurts so much, I know it well.

The degree of betrayal by a supposedly "so committed" partner who said that constantly like a lover.

Women speaking out against porn are silenced, since the public is desensitized and encouraged in it.

Arguing with him won't help. You'll get to the place (PTSD) of acceptance then transcend your personal hell.

The lady survivor said "he brought this filth into my beautiful life, he made my home a hell of lies/strife."

Major discovery realizing the degree to which they were living in a different reality from their frenemy.

Hypervigilance in relationship occurs because we need to feel safe and protect from deception again.

Hypervigilance: because she'll do anything to self-protect from having the rug pulled out again.

To save her more anguish he lies and deceives in little ways and this triggers her fear, insecurity even hate.

BETRAYAL TRAUMA

As survivors of porn addicts we must express ourselves for liberty, freedom and pursuit of happiness.

BETRAYAL TRAUMA SURVIVORS

Stop calling yourself a "codependent" but rather a betrayal trauma survivor, a real star.

Bottom line is nothing's changing. It's two steps up then five back, false promises but still shady.

Trauma bond is loyalty bond: your relationship thru time with someone who consistently hurts you.

So he had a bad childhood or learned it in the army--you're still the victim of his abusive behavior/treachery.

Cheating, disappearing, withholding attention, blowing hot and cold mixed with love nuggets of gold.

The intermittent reinforcements of highs and lows which he controls causes fixation, you've been sold.

With discovery of his secret sex life there's a flood of adrenalin which energizes us to escape the danger.

The Loyalty Bond is a drug addiction to the brain's chemical production with a vacillating environment.

With loyalty betrayal chemicals are released— must control/escape this with enforcing consequence and gaining distance.

PORN IS CHEATING

Pornography is cheating and it doesn't matter that chemicals can explain it--don't fall for it.

He did it, he did it again, he did it infinite times and will CONTINUE to, get that thru your mind.

BETRAYAL TRAUMA

For the real Betrayal Trauma comes from yourself—always thinking there is CHANGE when there is not.

He's mad at his wife for spying on him—well of course she is, he's into really weird evil stuff, AMEN?

"What can I do" the wife asks? When depleted, can't compete, given up, exhausted: pray/FAST.

The biggest trap is feeling sorry for the sinner. Don't get sucked in—you gotta keep truth front/center.

I don't dare to think things will work out as I[WE] want. I'm just moving point by point without a map.

It's hell living with a selfish sinner and to feel pity for him on top of it—plus wasting time. Tragic, lies.

The way you get to success is not to afflict people but to afflict self—fasting is the way, it's humbling.

I still feel the same as I did. If it be God's will it'll happen but I'm not banking my life on this dream.

And if something else comes up, well so be it.

To think by our relation I gotta have your alcoholism in my consciousness— that's the way life is.

Just by thinking of you I look down on myself. I can't have this—there's something about your matrix.

I gotta follow my FLOTUS on this: If you don't love me totally and only I will not give a mind to thee.

AFTER BETRAYAL TRAUMA

It's a chemical addiction to a person when you are trauma-bonded. It's very serious and I don't envy it.

BETRAYAL TRAUMA

The only way to break that bond [crazy loop] is to go no-contact THEN you start working on YOU.

I don't wanna eat. I wanna hurt. I don't know if this is masochism or the way this thing works.

I believe the only way to heal a broken heart is to fast, and losing faith in human nature starts a God-blast.

It went like this: Shocking discovery, hopes of recovery, repeated discovery then it became mundaneity.

Once it was my mundaneity it was a part of me. No good baby, must fast to return to factory settings: sanity.

His sin was a low level of. consciousness--the bottom of the barrel--and it brought disorder too/HELL.

I knew it was a chemical addiction--those chemicals from childhood trauma-- but could he lick them?

Every home has a different consciousness. Going to your house is like entering the third world, wtf miss?

So it's from childhood chemicals--does that mean he's not guilty? It may be the reason but so what baby.

So it's all explained chemically--does that mean he is guilt-free? Don't stay too much on this, stay free.

MESSY DISORDERLY HOMES

Going to hers is entering a not-quite clean and disorderly world of chaos, light years from my house.

I only want my home [utter concern for beauty and attention to detail] not yours, a bomb.

There are smells, there are things going on I don't know about, this is hell-- ESCAPE this right now.

BETRAYAL TRAUMA

Man's personality unfolds as he adapts to his environment. When it's sick he gets sick, when well, well.

And that is the function of the female: to make a HOME--establish environment--for man's unfoldment.

You've got her wrong. She substitutes/goes moot as a protection against ghosting--that's you.

One is from selfishness--the narcissist. The other is from the only reasonable self-defense, going silent.

It's all a matter of who goes moot/ghosts first. That's our virtual world so learn the patterns/manners.

He didn't go to better supply he went to someone who'd put up with his style much better, that's all.

And his STYLE is him getting admiration, that's all. He'll do anything for it including selling his soul.

Oh well the world is filled with em, he's just not your "Person". Dial him down, time to have fun.

He lost 100 lbs by [10] 90-hour fasts back to back with a 6000 calorie/three hour food window in between.

You may mal-adapt by giving up and taking the insane symptom for granted as normal: this is evil.

Forgive yourself for all insanity is immoral since it's from weak lines/no boundaries. We all sinned this way.

You're living with a sinner but then you think "we're all sinners" and here we go, back to indecision.

If I knew you [the link] was really there it'd be different for you know women, they need to be certain.

It's a matter of survival cuz its the weaker sex: must have certainty of supplies or could mean death.

BETRAYAL TRAUMA

BT: AN ONSLAUGHT OF BIOCHEMISTRY

Betrayal trauma is an onslaught of biochemistry that's beyond our control and attacks mind, body, soul.

Prioritize self-care with betrayal trauma: diet, sleep, meditation, keeping a list bringing certainty of his lusts.

Keep your concrete list handy so when the loyalty bonds kick in to make you deny it all, you're ready.

Learn about Intimate Partner Abuse, knowing it's all about brain chemicals and cutting him loose.

Remember that knowledge is power, so you are acting out of a knowing place.

It is so traumatizing to find out your husband wasn't who you thought he was.

Don't put so much energy into fixing this if he obviously isn't interested in his energy thus dispensed.

NOTHING IS SACRED TO THEM

Nothing is sacred to him who brings this filth into a happy home. You did everything, his substitute mom.

Jesus helps betrayal trauma cuz He knows all about fairweather friends and frenemies who lie/offend.

Why do we stay so long? It's the difficulty in reconciling who he IS with what we thought he was.

Always throwing me crumbs: he's still attracted to me, he can't live without me, he'll never love again, see?

Discovering what a pig he is releases the constant anxiety and that marks our victory, it's called D-Day.

It's priceless to not live with that horrific Relational Anxiety and Broken Loyalty Bonds in lying environments.

BETRAYAL TRAUMA

What fifty year old wants to compete with 20 year old strippers and porn stars? This was your life: war.

He has immediate attractions to people and you know it. It's magnetisms of the moment/you perceive it.

Betrayal trauma from discovering porn: Congratulations you've overcome the most insidious scorn.

Your new life starts the day you don't argue about this. You're in a new dimension, you see what it is.

WAITING FOR THE NEXT SHOE TO DROP

When is the next incident to happen? When will the other shoe drop? This has been tragic/I can't stop it.

You must accept in your heart he's not gonna stop seeking others. Always, your life and heart in tatters.

Millions of women are involved with profoundly character-disturbed cheaters and porn is their leader.

Porn is the same level of BETRAYAL as if the person was actually doing it--it's central to sex therapy.

It's the B.T's--Betrayal Trauma Jitteries

Intimacy Disorder: This explains attractions to OTHERS: to split off part of self and avoid who they are.

They keep a piece of themselves outside of their relationship, manifested in sexual porn or acting out.

Commitment-phobia is another way of saying: Intimacy Disorder. Keep a piece separate/go to others.

Five years is a long time to have your body in constant apprehension and fear. Betrayal Trauma/deep

BETRAYAL TRAUMA

Trauma is separation from self, others and society.

Porn is satanic and he's into it.

Strangely, we're more attracted to our abusive mates when kindness is mixed with pure abuse/sadness.

Change is painful, growth is painful and long but the worst is staying stuck where you don't belong.

The victim of betrayal trauma is not a "codependent" as if it's partly her fault. Get off of this you nut!

A SINGLE LIE DISCOVERY LEADS TO MYSTERY

A single lie discovered is enough creating doubt in every truth expressed. In an instant, happy home wrecked.

One lie discovered casts doubt on everything you say, man. Total fidelity in marriage, that's God's plan.

Threw me crumbs, felt relief which hooked me in. D-Day came (discovery) and I saw the devil/not my friend.

Anyone with a chronic cheater is low most of the time but goes wild with a few crumbs thrown, lies.

The loyalty bond is a drug addiction to the brain's chemical reaction to a vacillating environment.

He says "pornography isn't cheating". Not true, it's cheating of the worst kind and Jesus said it too.

He cheated on her constantly with the lust of his eyes--thinking of sex with every woman walking by.

Only by recovering from porn addiction can the culprit begin to see the collateral damage it caused.

Utah has the highest pornography rate and the highest plastic surgery rate-- wives competing with fate.

BETRAYAL TRAUMA

We're connected to someone who once felt safe like a lover but now it's horror, hurt and danger.

Due to morbid curiosity the cat is killed. He has no idea how it destroys his spouse when getting his fill.

Watch out for people who minimize porn. These are evil people telling you to adapt to it/just go on.

REJECT THOSE WHO MINIMIZE PORN

Betrayal Trauma therapy gets it--in concepts/words so you instantly understand the process and heal it.

Seeing Betrayal Trauma as anything but grief and loss you are not helpful. B.T. is hellish and horrible.

When you felt safety suddenly everything changes at the hands of he who was supposed to protect you.

After healing betrayal trauma any double message sets it in motion and it all comes back: can't trust him.

Yes, he's still the same guy--but the betrayed women then thinks that everything is a lie.

She takes every picture and marks "A" on his forehead--because she couldn't trust anything, all dead.

Being betrayed is like affecting your pc with a virus. The only way is to wipe it all out--what is real?

Pastor says "but he's a nice guy" and that's the end of it. Meanwhile she's in hell but can't explain it.

Betrayal Trauma in two stages: 1. Discovery. 2. She is now alone with it all cuz no one cares even he.

To "helpful" friends: It's not helpful to excuse unhealthy behaviors. You're making things worse/dangerous.

BETRAYAL TRAUMA

Forgiveness is releasing him to God. Trust takes a long time to rebuild, don't confuse these two.

Women betrayed by husbands feel isolated and doubt their personal worth-- similar to PTSD, a curse.

Recovery from Betrayal Trauma looks like an emotionally frenzied life full of fear cuz I've lost trust, dear.

NEED SAFETY TO BUILD INTIMACY

Safety is the foundation for rebuilding intimacy. If you don't feel it, distance yourself to stay happy.

If betrayal by a woman you know longer trust her in confidences important to you and then it is over.

Society is a hellish repetition of the meaningless and mundane. The inner journey is meaningful/sane.

Dense: Hypnotized by relationships.

The sinner is a double-minded man, unstable in all his ways.

Many forsake the saint/genius, loving the present world. Can you still trust God, rejected by boys and girls?

The reward for repentance is right-brain living--a magical, charmed life: synchronicity/no strife.

That's the trick: Though family and friends detest, to pass the test and be the best in whom all now invest.

Creative genius comes out in work you love. You'll be aghast at scary human dramas thick as mud.

MORE ON NARCISSISTS

The narcissist takes what you gave him and spreads it around as if it's all from him, expect it friend.

BETRAYAL TRAUMA

I only want a man who loves only me and brings me protection and stability. That's IT for me.

With him in your life you're eclipsed and look down on yourself but now you're back, fully endowed.

With him in your life you're always in competition but without him it's a psychic assassination.

Boom: just like that and the problem is over for good. Just don't go back because it's all understood.

As long as you're other-directed, the curse is him not seeing your worth. You must now be first.

Another time or place we woulda been a perfect match but can't you see we're in a crosshatch?

I compete with no one and if not **NUMBER ONE** I'll escape the painful matrix surrounding your narc harem.

If I'm not **NUMBER ONE** it's f-you, GTH, disconnect, never see you again, get away from me you twit.

I think you are a liar and expect demeaning sexual acts from women. This makes you vermin!

I expect nothing else from you now so the hurt is gone. I'm in a whole other sphere, from the coop I've flown.

THEY CAN'T HIDE WHO THEY ARE

And you can't hide who you are either, I sense duplicity a mile away and don't like what I'm feeling brother.

So that's it--he's gone. Your higher self protected your inner child for once and now it's a new song.

"I'm stuck in the muck and can't get out--please help!" Keep praying, focus, **KNOW** you want OUT.

BETRAYAL TRAUMA

You don't HAVE to be treated like this. It's demeaning, off-putting, makes you hate yourself every day.

I agree you clog my lines. The work gets static in it suddenly--that's the bad influence of swine.

I'd rather be with an oldster who hasn't swum in those muddy waters or has overcome the culture.

You wanna keep one foot in, one foot out to keep your fans stimulated but that won't work, it's a turn off.

I can't/won't compete, I'm gonna enjoy the non-competitive atmosphere I've created: home life of an elite.

I wish you the best but I'm just not interested. There's no reason to be, I've got my own destiny you see.

You say too many cultural things that indicate you are too worldly for me. I just can't relate/I can't compete.

CRUELIANS

Careful who you put your faith in--who you associate with--since the influence is there with mere contact.

The shark knows this: his sequence is contact, influence, CONQUEST.

Conquest is over your mind which ceases to be a lovely garden/starry night and starts being a scene from hell.

When to bad influences you caved you made wrong decisions which degraded your life for decades.

Dissociating from lower elements is the name of the game--separate to re-connect to power and fame.

Popularity means nothing--or do you think just cuz they're accepted you should put your faith in them?

BETRAYAL TRAUMA

Falling into the popular groove they're out of grace and will only misadvise you on what you should do.

Tragedies from bad influences: scary to realize this but incredibly beneficial to open to beautiful future!

Thinking most people are "nice" is very stupid--stay alert to subtle influences tearing you down, stricken.

Misplaced faith inspires fear which is instinct warning of possible destruction--powerlessness felt in stomach.

Faith in an unstable man is like living on quicksand. From highest highs to devastating lows, oh man.

Dulling instincts to avoid recognition of creeps: are you stuffing/drinking down fears on a road so steep?

Become aware of/question associates. You're blocked and you need silence to succeed not games/noise.

Their loyalty is divided between God and the world, and they are unstable in everything they do. James 1: 8

Keep chatterers (using you for entertainment) at bay for these are energy thieves and time is late.

SINS ARE MAL-ADAPTIVE COPING DEVICES

Sins are coping devices to adapt to people in your environment. Man is an adaptive animal/you're mal-adaptive.

Exhaustion is the result of oppression--from letting inferiors worm their way in.

Since hostile environments are sterile dynasties/petty competition, they contaminate/restrict creation.

Dense environments are based on rules you want no part of. Your destiny is genius without map or plan.

BETRAYAL TRAUMA

Study the ways to escape cruel people then life comes together as hypnotic spells of all systems dissolve.

Now you see the mixed signals keeping you down rather than the blame and shame from their game.

Study the subtleties of human cruelties so you can shake loose from the denial of bad faith tragedies.

Detachment from fruitless relationships brings explosion into new wonderlands--detach then open up, man!

One's Self has been defined against these grounds so detach so that God brings these traitors down.

The wonderful release from people is ineffable as the past's heartbreak dissolves to joy/self-control.

Detach so now the universe and God--the lovely moment--defines you. The joyous release is ineffable!

As long as you keep thinking about past creeps they're still defining you and you sink in your swill and stew.

Cruelty is too subtle, silent and insidious to see and thus we only hear of love/goodness, masks of the unfree.

Cruelty is rarely mentioned since as a sinister force it prevents its own exposure and we're less for it.

Learning about subtle cruelty liberates you with perfect protection so learn them for it happens fast, man.

I recall the pains: broken promises/plans, being stood up/kept waiting, gossip-called-concern, a hostile stare.

PERVERSE TRIANGLES/SECRET ALLIANCES

Cruelty: perverse triangles/secret alliances, sarcasm, dangerous advice or casual misjudgments.

BETRAYAL TRAUMA

There is active cruelty then passively witnessing or allowing it to occur--in both it's an invisible empire.

Cruelty registers deep, resulting in addictions to avoid anxiety as a pervasive anger takes over.

Denial keeps us hooked to the cruel effects while awareness though painful gives protection/prevention.

Cruelty doesn't leave by ignoring it for like cancer it grows more menacing under the surface, believe it.

See the light to avoid a fight. It's ignorance of cruelty that maintains it and awareness makes it right.

It is good to see the wild wickedness of people for then our great work blossoms and we reap, filled.

Cruelty is subtle so catch it before it clips you. Become as skilled as identifying stars and always see truth.

You must think: "she said that to get revenge" or "he did that to make me jealous cuz he can't control me."

No need to confront cruelty--just seeing it stamps out denial/anger. You're now free as the lone ranger.

Despite "loving" image this generation isn't nice as we witness pure hypocrisy and the cruelian is hurt mostly.

The cruelian's first victim is himself since he hates truth and decency as different from him--really creepy.

Some people love getting you into trouble. Stay clear for a chief cause of sorrow is blindness to evil.

THE BLIND INSIST THEY CAN SEE

The worst part is the blind insisting they can see. Who does this remind you of, the liberals ya' think?

BETRAYAL TRAUMA

The unhappy climate with a cruelian is marked by frequent fickleness/explosions of suppressed anger.

Had you just known! Learn from that to avoid annoying involvements to which your center says "NO.".

Notice how quickly people change their minds: friendly and helpful then cold, evasive and unkind.

Are your protectors your worst enemies? Don't be dismayed--sad realizations mark growth into maturity.

Let the tears flow then open to the future and oceans of power. You've always known but denial dulls/sours.

Face human haze to get high prize of those set apart from the maize--the misjudgments of masked identities.

No friends = success.

Dare to see through weakness posing as strength for staying in delusion is heartbreaking for the saints.

Growing up is giving up foolish fantasies about inefficient diets, phony friends and fallacious family fakes.

The more familiar the pain caused by persecutors the deeper the knife—perhaps for your whole life.

You're so used to it you can't think straight anymore! A release about to occur--no more sucker for mockers.

TAKE CONTROL: DELETE FOOLS/CHOOSE FOLKS

To be champ, delete fools/choose your folks. You must never rely on immature souls pulling the rug out.

As you learn to stand alone you will surely feel much safer with just truth and God as your teacher.

BETRAYAL TRAUMA

A cruel act is an explosion of suppressed energy. The pressure accumulates from foes smelling like a rose.

An inwardly wrong person is under the pressure of this conflict which regularly erupts causing pain/damage.

When truth finally takes inner hold, cruelians lose pressure from pretense and thus cruelty also goes.

The phony ain't fine so you gotta draw that line. He is gross and un-free: it's his envy you must flee.

The greater your role shall be, the better you'll feel as just "me". People are just an encumbrance, see?

Law of affinity says things of like tone vibrate together. Attractions or repulsions based on behavior.

Wrongness hates rightness so the two can never relate--they walk different paths of love vs. hate.

It helps to know the faker of right is always wrong.

Getting hurt by wrong people reflects denied wrong in ourselves attracted to weakness posing as strength.

The phony is blindly attracted to phoniness. They deserve each other so let em go and find godliness.

Be internally right to receive the safety of that rightness by avoiding the toxic system, your highness!

See it for God's sake--for a romance or friendship with a cruelian is like living with a rattlesnake!

LIVING WITH A RATTLESNAKE

See the truth as a guide in all male-female relations then everything becomes smooth and pleasant.

BETRAYAL TRAUMA

No wrong man can hurt a right woman by instinct alone/no wrong woman deceives a righteous man who knows.

Lord turned captivity of Job when he prayed for his friends so let's pray: "please Lord help these phonies."

Most common fear is their anger. Knowing the nutty nasty nature of humans deletes fear/leads you higher.

Prince will no longer tremble before rabble. Only the weak wear wrath, yet you weep? No more, you're able.

Declare independence, stay safe and human storms will be of non-effect save resentments from the past.

If you can understand, you command. By giving up delusions your inner journey expands into God's plan.

DETACH FROM THE OUTER

Detach from the outer, implode to the inner just by skipping dinner and avoiding the controlling sinner.

Never knew I was mimicking mom the shrew. My apologies to Chuck, Danny, Dwight, Richard, Jimmy and Ray too.

Declare independence, stay safe and human storms will be of non-effect save resentments I'd expect.

What built this country was not rolling over but attacking the enemy.

Cruelians love the thrill of hurting others. Playing games and repeating templates confirms his greatness.

Just when you're happy he falls into his bag: keeping you waiting, forcing you into hardship/irritation.

We've all been attacked: he's making you jealous/feel less, old, unholy, a phony and you buy that crap.

BETRAYAL TRAUMA

He digs driving you to desperation and that's the power you give him--so just by learning, you win.

Dare to disappoint demanders--never give what you don't want to give. Beware of expectations: abusive.

DARE TO DISAPPOINT DEMANDERS

Discern the valuable from the worthless--egotistical cruelians have no value to you my dearest.

Becoming alert to the harmful or unpleasant builds instincts of the mind as well as boundaries and habit.

No more denial, now you're alert: a rich squirt free of hurts and neurotic quirks cuz you didn't come first.

The cruelian thinks for you--like Elmer Fudd. Refuse the charlatan's two cents and think as you should.

Involvement with wrong can distract/delete decades from God's plan so take control with perfect protection.

"What are you really like behind the mask?" Since he knows he's false he'll either flee or attack.

See that nice lady? She's really a scorpion. Fakery is the cause of cruelty so escape hurt be seeing the shady.

Cruelians are conquistadors--compelled to win the debate, score the ego point, be a hero--so shut the door!

Instead of deflation think: "this could have been handled in a higher way." So why settle for the lower, ok?

The conquering fool is low lured by like-lowness. He can never see the higher world, not knowing himself.

He wants his wicked ways to work in sin and hates you for your foolish flattery of a fake like him, a no-win.

BETRAYAL TRAUMA

The fool tries to please the cruelian thinking he'll be loved but becomes weak declaring cruelty is a dove.

CREEPY CRUELIANS ONLY BRING YOU DOWN

Why reward the ruinous, the recalcitrant, the rank? The creepy cruelian can only bring you down: no thanks.

Some fear rejecting misery-makers thinking they need these stinkers. Detach to be true clear thinkers!

It's your awareness alone subduing haters but your blind denial is the glue of gossiping collaborators.

For the cure take a one month bipolar (IN-OUT) diet to weed your friendships who are lying about it.

People are either IN or OUT. The INs you love, adore, cherish and reward, the OUTs you avoid, reject, ignore.

The outs can't hurt you again once you become the master for it was you sending invitations for disaster.

Practice IN and OUT for more relief than you've ever known. No more slights for the King knows the foe.

Keep your head above the cruel crowd through aristocratic reserve. Be terse, laconic, sober--observe.

The down-and-outs hate you for placating, pandoring to and pleading with their sick, silly and sadistic souls.

Cruelians only love those seeing through them so designate him OUT to bring respect precursory to love.

Make people win your favor by growing up, while never trying to win their favor again just the Lord above.

THEY ARE EITHER "IN" OR "OUT"

BETRAYAL TRAUMA

Your new matrix of **IN-OUT** is a new future for the relief from tension opens the floodgates energy for sure.

Since all misjudgment is oppressive the **IN-OUT** matrix removes the block keeping you from success.

Sweet silence says it all--they know what they did anyway so there is nothing to say, just stand tall.

Your golden silence is a siren suggesting they spurt up speedily or "so long, so-low, I'm going solo."

Bringing up the bad past--labels and fables--is a sign of manipulation since Jesus said it is over.

Cruelians love bringing up your (bad) past. Think "ABM": Attack Bad Memories of events that are passed.

Cruelians seek to weaken/confuse you to inflate self but you aren't that person, the true self is reinventin'.

Call a rattlesnake a "kitten" and it's still what it is. Ignore self-flattering labels and just see realities.

Liberals, democrats and dam rats call themselves "loving" to veil viciously vindictive minds.

It's the "humanitarian" groups hogging/hoarding power/wealth so question the popular you love so much.

Cruelians always excuse brutality—they've a right to attack, betray a promise or rub your nose in the past.

When he justifies, he lies. Worse, his cronies support hypocrisy while his victims call him charming.

DETACH THROUGH A SECRET WORLD

To detach, live in your own secret world. We can't change em but can detach thru our journey inward.

BETRAYAL TRAUMA

Solitude is the mistress to turn to when people problems persist then enjoy the ecstasy of living highest.

Never let em know how childish/ignorant they are. Keep wisdom in your secret world then become a star.

Living in desert solitude I turn turn from man, mass or mess to face the beautiful mountain vistas in bliss.

In the miraculous moment all goes "strangely dim." Everyone's on probation with me cuz I see only eternity.

Phony friends/fickle family contaminated your aura so rise outa reach through regality: just God and thee.

Turn to eternity when all people problems have passed. Think, dream, plan for the future glories so vast!

The cruelian is a pouncer looking for an excuse to scream, attack and injure-- his cold eyes make you unsure.

Pain of persecution dissolves when you see the incredible pressure between the true self and the facade.

They explode with "polite" cruelties as a bio-device to release blocked energy- -don't fear, just get insight.

Perception prevents pain while denial allows cruelians to confuse, cajole and cause you to cringe.

The weak talk too much/can't understand why you'd rather think than talk. Let them go the dumb rocks.

Even if you have to live with animals alone, at least you'll get your work done.

After separating it will be effortless. See the divine design then it's a case of beauty from ashes.

THE DEVIL'S CROWD IS POLITICALLY CORRECT

BETRAYAL TRAUMA

The devil's crowd is politically correct. They tow the line saying whatever's popular but not the Elect.

The weak talk constantly, habitually and idly. The biggest drain on genius and reason for boredom, surely.

The weak are so dependent on you they'll come without calling first, Draw a line for privacy or be cursed.

You must manage people now. Your work is deep and intricate, they must shut their mouths or GET OUT.

Tyranny of the group wants you down and hopeless making you prove yourself creating more embarrassment.

Say "I can't deal with your projections nor talk again." Overcome subtle yet pervasive obstacles: use assertion.

The dominator adapted to your docility so be assertive baby then new attractions = success, truly.

Just BE right so no more memories, habits or systems take hold. Be like all saints in history: BOLD.

Gossip can't hurt you--it's just a name/label. You've grown weary so declare independence then bye, Mabel.

When you're out of the system there's nothing they can do so keep saying when down: case closed, whew!

You've been infected but now you'll be better, then best--release this system and transcend to your crest.

ENDING WITH NO FRIENDS IS BEST

If upon waking to the abuse you find yourself without friends, great--you'll now be with God, the highest.

God knows your great future--this present situation is part of your training: unforgettable/heartbreaking.

BETRAYAL TRAUMA

As you come to your talents remember this: jealousy is their incentive: Make you small/not get so big.

Choice: Faith in wrong people (bad faith) or experience true fullness, for bad faith makes you depressed.

There's no happiness with bad faith as the contradictions are a cancer to the subconscious, ok?

When the tension of denial is gone you're back in the Kingdom: your center, your home.

Acceptance reached brings reversal: you're now in a joyful light so be assertive with many rehearsals.

These people putting painful projections on you care nothing for your joy.

We have a choice: Bad faith or true fullness. Bad faith brings depression while the truth creates happiness.

BAD FAITH IN USELESS PEOPLE

Bad faith in useless people through denial results in dulled eyes/dense brain and dimmed experience.

With them around to stay you have flagged interest in destiny and projects-- you don't cherish the day.

Everything forced unconscious makes us dense, as our projects dim anytime we deny the obvious.

Bad relationships degrade reality--the hard-won bud of genius. This beautiful seed is smashed by this.

Once the light goes out due to carnal/vulgar or indifferent your creativity is ruined by these children.

When they hear less than 90% get asylum they'll be incentivized to crash the border/more following.

BETRAYAL TRAUMA

True pleasure is blocked by tension so release prideful people/pastimes and find fullness: ecstasy in life.

True pleasure is blocked by tension, so release prideful people/pastimes and find fullness, a mansion.

HOME CENTER SOLUTION: SOLITUDE

We lose identity when enmeshed in groups, mal-adapting by dropping parts of self then being duped.

We should be moving to a more independent reality, not a more enmeshed one then getting silly.

Independence is the discoverer who splits from the majority view which everyone knows is "true".

High boundaries is an essential achievement for success to occur--separation precedes success for sure.

An anorexic undifferentiated early from the family system compensates by going opposite later--total reclusion.

In solitude she learns petty competition/jealousies are instantly dissolved with her total inaccessibility.

Tho' she was a "blank slate" for others projections she's now warm steel-- impervious, cordial but firm.

The female overcomer jealously guards who's around for it is "contact, influence, conquest."

Children love non-competitive games the most: it is independence that brings genius expression/BOSS.

Happiest cultures are non-competitive and genius competes with no one--for in his unique stream there is none.

Competitive groups ruin genius thus rare talent secludes, never compares with others, keeps to himself.

BETRAYAL TRAUMA

Your essence is your private castle for nothing else compares. Home-centered is SELF-centered, rare.

If your home doesn't reflect you, you lack center and are owned by society. And the dirt and clutter, oh my.

Uncentered: home is in shambles while they travel with the rabble.

YOUR ESSENCE IS YOUR PRIVATE CASTLE

Regain center to feel the wonderful joy of knowing the YOU as distinguished from the masses/whew.

Selfishness/domination is described as tolerance/liberation and degeneracy is described as "freedom".

Conspiring to open our borders to foreign invasion--THAT is the biggest charge to Obama of treason.

The non-competitive atmosphere of your home transcends time and space so become inaccessible, please!

Stay home, choose your experience, make your home reflect your personality and never adapt again!

Choose ALL as you simultaneously seclude. Love your little niche, fill time with solitary pursuits and get rich.

Through the inner journey you gain discernment and high boundaries defining True Royalty, finally.

The opposite of royalty is being emotionally dependent on a vacillator who breaks your heart!

It's the science of silence vs. codependence with a lush or louse.

If one is right then silence is the most perfect way to deal with resistance.

Until one's time has come, fighting resistance only tore him down but surety, silence and seclusion won.

BETRAYAL TRAUMA

GROUPS MAD AT ME: LOYALTY OR AUTONOMY?

In groups loyalty/protection transcends autonomy/self-realization so they always side against the great ones.

Groups: Denial of self combined with mutual consideration are more esteemed than expression of Self.

For genius there is sanctity to separation and seclusion until his time has come to catalyze the nation.

Be a genius in your field (release into cosmic freedom) or endure the horrors of codependency, dumbed.

Here the dominant one maintains superiority by "advising" then getting angry with independent striving.

Anger inspires fear leading to bad faith/lost fullness. With growth the dominant lay traps but then fall into it.

PUTTING FAITH WHERE IT BELONGS

Put your faith where it belongs: in your own stream and instincts for then God protects your moments.

"Holy" means separate, like God—to be holy is to be separate. Because God is separate, holy is non-ordinary.

Highest religious experience is reflecting divine, so separate/insulate so God shines thru talents refined.

Finish work then rest. A period of "ecstatic rest" is your last phase and for new royalty, rest precedes rule, ok?

I apologize to every male I knew since 14. I was in denial while mimicking my mother who was angry, see?

My military husband wouldn't take it so laid the law down. I got my ears back suddenly, I was in love.

BETRAYAL TRAUMA

It's a **CLICK** in the head when you fall into line. No more whine/the arrogance of ego both yours and mine.

Deceivers cause confusion from his anxious face, resentful words and empty life--Lord, I need space!

CRUELIANS LOVE PUTTING YOU IN FEAR

He puts you in fear as his defeats are your worries. Let this be your blessing for visions spring from crises.

Use the cruelian's terrible traumas and tantrums to reveal solutions while giving you the will to act on them.

God doesn't want you destroyed by evil--only seeing through people brings joy, no more feeble but gleeful!

Ask: "do I want to be here with him/them? Success comes with seeing through the world's false front/"fun".

They do wrong cuz they don't know right so always remember the higher conquers the lower.

Unconsciously they act superior assuming the pecking order is right and you are wrong--social hypnotism.

Don't struggle to win, let God come down on him. It's society vs. God who is on your side and friend.

Never expect compassion from a cruelian unless it's part of his game, remembering he'll change.

Stand in high silence so high science can make his effect null and void. Don't engage and even avoid.

Test the cruelian's terror from being ignored and watch as the hurtful hero cries like a baby's tantrum.

Your denial of what he's really like means one thing: the sly sadist succeeds in leading you to strife and sadness.

BETRAYAL TRAUMA

Has this not occurred all through your past? You deny, you cry. You buy that lie, then to self-esteem: bye-bye.

Superior insight: Don't fear labels for now you can read people in a new way no matter what their image.

HARD-HEARTED ARE MISERABLE/CRUEL ARE LOST

The hard-hearted are miserable, the cruel are lost and the touchy have only pretensions of happiness.

The vicious or vile masochistically prefer self-destructive attacks over a peaceful existence. Vernon Howard

Self-destruction is a painful thrill and the harder they fall (e.g. in love) the quicker they'll turn on you.

When trust is lost, it is lost. Some sneaks are snakes, striking then slithering away for good then you're boss.

Superior insight is the ability to see the reversals and ferocious flip-flops of people: friendly then evil.

OP-TRUTH: all men are two (opposite) people in one as there are two brains and separate nervous systems.

The private and social sides are worlds apart. To deny it you comparmentalize it then soon there is disaster.

For stability in hostile environments think: "it's a package deal" then as Jekyll becomes Hyde, decide.

CAREFUL OF EVIL HELPERS

You get their help but soon you'll yelp. Calmly take note then take a new boat.

If you don't know cruelians this may seem negative. But even you will feel people pain or witness it.

Now you've a peaceful view. With a new mind you see the connection between fear and behavior towards you.

BETRAYAL TRAUMA

Anxiety attracts hurt you believe the harsh can inflict but understanding breaks the power of the witch.
Brutal man cries he's changed his ways, appeases with apologies then strikes again. His cries are lies/no friend.

Though a snake learns to kiss he's still a snake. Catch cunning cruelty by asking: is it ego or truth?

Since truth doesn't deceive you know conceit caused the cruelty and exposure makes it powerless, so believe.

Cruel gang demands you plan for their benefit so casually ignore and plan your own right life without em.

Stay free of psychic violence as an anger-detective: sudden silence, sly sarcasm, sullen stares, silly submission.

Anger signs: forced jocularity and coldly polite accusations--now detach from bad memories or emotions.

STRIFE IS A KILLER

Whether it comes from sugar or bad history, strife is a killer: a demon sent from hell to ruin destiny.

Strife is malice, envy, jealousy, anger, resentment and bitterness. It comes thru sin--of act or association.

Strife means lost meaning and anointing (presence of God) and spiritual gifts are gone with the rifts.

Remember: The cruelian wants to involve us in strife so we must do everything but go to war if we have to.

Stress-based diseases from strife: to the nervous system, organs, and tissues it's like a knife.

Resentments cause disease from asthma to warts. Know why then disease departs.

BETRAYAL TRAUMA

Cruelian is conflicted, you were the closest victim, period. Wisdom is your shield but denial = no power to wield.

For attention bullies behave brutally to be fearfully noticed with screams or arguments so don't do it.

SPIN DOCTORS AND PLASTIC SURGEONS

All's a fraud in the era of spin-doctors and plastic surgeons. Superficial matters and character is lost.

It's not what things are but what they appear to be. Machiavelli

Everything depends on perceptions and what matters most is the first impression.

You have character--who you are when no one sees--while the double-minded is unstable in all his ways.

Take the day to think back to all the miracles God did for you, building the faith you need for success too.

NOT MULTICULTURAL, ONE BIG BROWN BLOB

They don't want multicultural but mono-culture: one big brown blob that they define and it's vulgar.

With gate locked they can't knock on your door. You might let em in and then they'd block and bore.

Character wins out/falseness fails as an overnight success crashes as hype/spin dies without leaving a trail.

Start the diet of freedom having banished all distractions from your purpose-work without these burdens.

God's wisdom is all you need to transcend your weird world. Fools hate knowledge, prepare for scorn.

The world's wisdom and God's are opposites, so learn to savor sweet saintly solitude and like me, LOVE IT.

BETRAYAL TRAUMA

Well you've seen the light and now you have no friends! Don't fret just get to know God as life mends.
You're in training--God knows your future. Jealousy brings anger: they made you feel small/you were in danger.

They want power over you to compensate their lowness in comparison, so witchcraft takes over nation.

SUPERIOR PAST TIMES

The most evocative past times are music and our yard. The magnificent views then back to the bard.

Most profitable work comes from not-working but when triggered you can't stop working until completing.

Got a profitable weekend planned: music, movies and sitting out in the sun/with view, getting ideas.

God said "what am I gonna do to get you to stop working? I say to you: take a vacation it's much more worthy."

End of 48 hour fast. Now do I eat when not hungry or just take a nap? I'll extend the fast, think I'll do that.

Most profitable past time: doing nothing. No distractions, truth uncovering. Stop working/start improving.

Most profitable past time: old movies, loved music, counting our blessings, not eating.

Well goodbye we're off for our four-day weekend. When every day's a Saturday--that kind of thinking.

I sense duplicity with a neighbor. Instead of frantic gift giving to repair why not use the best: prayer.

I'm off for my weekend vacation of music, movies and sunning: a mental transport without leaving.

BETRAYAL TRAUMA

Fav music: downtempo lounge jazz. Fav movie: The Great Sinner. Fav past time: looking out the winder.

I came from Southern California: orange juice and tacos was my sustenance thru adolescence.

The Grapecure is the Diet of Last Resort. Two weeks to live and yet them come back, fresh start.

YOU'LL MOVE RIGHT ON

So you played out a Janis Joplan archetype--so what. It was a lesson in psychology, just forget it.

All writers are vain, selfish and lazy. Exploring the basis of that is pure mystery. George Orwell

I gotta work until the end and I only wanna live here in my beautiful mansion viewing the red mountains.

HIX POLITIX: BLAME IT ALL ON US
Biggest Betrayal Trauma of All,
Since Our People Built this Country

The average white person is a virtue signaling liberal who's on another planet. Alex Jones

I can't bear to hear about statues anymore. An historical wasteland without national self-worth.

Must have a break from politics and current events. Need R and R or I get too nervous--music LIFTS.

GAME PLAN: Their only way to free Black America is to destroy white supremacy that rules our land.

Like South Africa, no appeasement will ever be enough. This is a Race War and we'd better get tough.
Already the most persecuted creature is the White Man and that will unfortunately trigger them.

BETRAYAL TRAUMA

The local liberal leaders are totally caving in and even helping them pursue nihilistic destruction.

Race-baiting and liberal thinking is always about putting one up and the other down/it's all around.

What I most wanted was to turn political writing into an art. George Orwell

THUGS BRINGING US TO CRISIS

If we don't stop the thugs from bringing us to crisis the tanks will roll in and that'll be normalized: ugh.

It's all come home to roost. The crap we're enduring now is the culmination of three generations making fools.

You don't have to apologize for crimes you did not commit. We're about the individual not the group you twit.

When you muffle yourself cuz there's things you can't say you weaken your character/more controllable.

To combat a system permeated with lies you must never lie about anything, not one thing. Jordan Peterson

If fed on lies the world hits back without meaning, then one is bitter, resentful, murderous/genocidal.

Totalitarianism, if not fought against, can triumph anywhere and that's why we stay vigilant of disorder.

In this new world we're approaching there will be only fear, rage, triumph, self-debasement. George Orwell

KAREN KELLOCK PH.D.

M.S. Political Science, San Diego State. Ph.D. in Psychology, University of California Irvine. Postdoctoral: UCI School of Medicine, Dept. of Psychiatry [NIMH Grants]. Developed the Debris Theory of Disease, a theory of system pathology in 120 books and 22 textbooks for the general public. The theory has a general formula: All disease is obstruction, all recovery is elimination, all success is attraction. The three obstructions are people, habit and food. Remove obstruction and snap to your goals, waiting in the wings.

www.ingramcontent.com/pod-product-compliance
Lightning Source LLC
Chambersburg PA
CBHW061714250726
48657CB00002B/618